# SPIRITUALLY HEALING

### THE

# INDIGO CHILDREN

(and Adult Indigos, Too!)

JODERE

GROUP

SAN DIEGO, CALIFORNIA

# SPIRITUALLY HEALING

## THE

# INDIGO CHILDREN

(and Adult Indigos, Too!)

### THE PRACTICAL GUIDE AND HANDBOOK

◆ ◆ ◆

Wayne Dosick, Ph.D.
Ellen Kaufman Dosick, MSW

JODERE GROUP, INC.
P.O. Box 910147
San Diego, CA 92191-0147
www.jodere.com

*Book design by Charles McStravick*
*Editorial supervision by Chad Edwards*

The authors of this book do not dispense medical advice or prescribe the use of any techniques as forms of treatment for physical, medical, emotional, or spiritual problems for you or your child without you seeking the advice of a physician or mental health professional, either directly or indirectly. The intent of the authors is only to offer information of a general nature to help you in your quest for emotional and spiritual well-being. In the event you use any of the information in this book for yourself, which is your constitutional right, the authors and the publisher assume no responsibility for your actions.

**CIP data available from the Library of Congress**

ISBN 1-58872-088-8

07 06 05 04   4 3 2 1
First printing, May 2004

PRINTED IN THE UNITED STATES OF AMERICA

for

SEGGY & DOOGLA

*Who bring us back to the Garden,*
*inspire us to remember,*
*and hold for us the vision of Eternal Eden.*

# CONTENTS

# ACKNOWLEDGMENTS

We are deeply and humbly grateful to:

- ◆ God and Guidance who called us to this sacred mission, and our teachers, mentors, rebbes, and guides who have brought us to this moment.

- ◆ Our friends and colleagues Nancy Ann Tappe, Jan Tober, Lee Carroll, and Dr. Doreen Virtue who were the first to see and serve the Indigo Children.

- ◆ The children and their parents who graciously participated in our early research, and began calling us "The YOUMEE People."

- ◆ The thousands of Indigo Children and their parents, and Adult Indigos, who have had the faith to come into the World of the Spirit, and have felt the power—and the life-blessing— of these spiritual healings.

- ◆ The scores of women and men who have—and will—become Certified Facilitators of The Soul Center for Spiritual Healing, and will bring these Spiritual healings to Indigos all over the globe.

- ◆ Debbie Luican and her extraordinary colleagues at Jodere Group, who are celebrating Spirit, and brilliantly paradigm-shifting the world of publishing. We are proud to be part of their vision.

♦ Cecilia Schulberg and Jessica Schulberg, Heather Petrek and Zachary Petrek, and David Rafsky, whose images grace these pages, and who most lovingly shared with us the goodness and the grandeur of their Spirit; and Shendl Diamond, whose delicate calligraphy flows from the depths of her sweet soul.

♦ And most, the Indigo Children, whom we are honored to serve, and whose vision of a world of goodness and perfection dances before us. We pray and strive for the day when every Human Being embraces and embodies the Indigo-eternal-teaching of peace and love. Then, all will be One. Then, Earth will be Eden.

We are not human beings having a spiritual experience.

We are spiritual beings having a human experience.

— Pierre Teilhard de Chardin

You
are
Children
of
Spirit

# THESE ARE OUR CHILDREN

## Who Are the Indigo Children?

If you have picked up this book, it may well be that you have an **Indigo Child.**

If so, you know the Indigo Children well.

**More than 80 percent of the children now being born are Indigo Children.**

If you could see their energy fields (and we know that some of you can!), you would see a beautiful deep blue color in their fields.

That is why they are called "Indigos."

**Our Indigos are a "new breed" of children, here to help transform this world.**

Your Indigo Child—along with millions of other Indigos:

- ♦ Is immensely likable and endearing.

- ♦ Is highly intelligent, deeply intuitive, incredibly creative, full of energy.

- ♦ Is self-reliant and self-sufficient.

- ♦ Has high self-esteem, and an almost-regal sense of entitlement.

- ♦ Usually "gets it" before anyone else, and has little patience for rules or authority or "old" structures.

◆ Is a "wise old soul" with a keen sense of purpose and destiny.

◆ Seems to carry with him/her eternal remembering, and holds a vision of joyful, harmonious perfection for our world.

And at the same time, he or she may *also* seem:

◆ Uneasy "in his skin"; uncomfortable in his life; unhappy being here on Earth.

◆ Extremely sensitive and reactive to everything from someone else's mood, to world events, to food, to the general feel of the environment.

◆ As if she is in deep emotional pain, and, sometimes in high anxiety and distress.

◆ To do poorly at school, and be overly-aggressive—or withdrawn—at play.

◆ To often "act out," and have trouble "fitting in" and "getting along" at home and at school.

◆ To sometimes "play out" his anguish in more serious anti-social attitudes and behaviors, and to have difficulty knowing the difference between right and wrong.

◆ To feel her own pain, but not know how to cope.

Hundreds of thousands, perhaps millions, of our Indigo Children have been labeled ADD or ADHD or ODD. And hundreds of thousands are being given prescription drugs to hopefully ease their discomfort, and so that they will be easier to "manage" and "control."

If these descriptions seem to fit your child(ren), we know that while you rejoice in the magnificent Being your child is, and celebrate his uniqueness, and delight in her humor, and marvel at his creativity, you may also be at your wit's end, wondering if the "emotional roller-coaster" that your children—and you with them—are on will ever end.

We understand that you are tired of the phone calls from the school, and the disapproving glances from strangers, and designing your entire family's activities around your Indigo's moods, behaviors, and needs. And we know that you often feel frustrated and sad at the obvious frustration and sadness that your child is feeling.

You may have already tried some of the dozens of worthy and valuable suggestions offered by grandparents, teachers, coaches, therapists, clergy, doctors, child specialists, and writers about nutrition, behavior modification, exercise, environment, medication, and school advocacy. And some of the advice may have been helpful. And yet you may still be watching your Indigo Child suffering deep within him/herself.

Our Indigos are here on this Earthplane because they have so much to contribute and share in this world. It is hard to see their pain and discomfort get in the way of their magnificence shining through—and truly not know how to help.

## Spiritual Guidance Guides

Our Spiritual Guidance teaches that our Indigo Children come to Earth **holding a vision of a perfected world.**

**Their great pain comes from the dissonance they feel between their vision, and the wildly imperfect world they see and experience.**

**Their pain is at a spiritual, emotional, energetic—soul—level.**

And, therefore, the healing for their pain must come from that same spiritual, emotional, energetic—soul—level.

## Spiritual Healing

How does spiritual healing happen?

**There are seventeen spiritual woundings** that children can experience. So, our Guidance has given us seventeen corresponding little healing games that children—between the ages of seven and seventeen—and their parents play, using words and movements to act on the spiritual—the soul—level in order to bring healing.

We call the processes *"The 17."*

# THE 17
## Spiritually Healing Children's Emotional Wounds

The little games are called **"YOUMEES,"** because they are done between "you" and "me," the child and the parent. These healings "drain away" the energy from the emotional wounds, and without the energetic power to propel them, the woundings heal.

The YOUMEES are exquisite. Each one takes no longer than two minutes to play, is fun, and has an emotional impact on both children and parents.

And, better yet, **parents report swift and dramatic changes in children's attitudes and behaviors.** They watch their children's emotional pain and spiritual angst diminish, and their lives become more comfortable and happy.

## FOR CHILDREN YOUNGER THAN 7

What about the little ones, your children who are **younger than age seven?**

It is both spiritually and cognitively difficult for children under the age of seven to follow the YOUMEE instructions.

But happily, our little ones do not have to be left in emotional pain.

There is a spiritual healing process for Indigo children from birth to age seven, where the parent surrogates, or acts, on behalf of the child.

It is called:

# GRACELIGHT
## Weaving Harmony for the Littlest Indigos

## For Children—and Adults—Older Than 17

And what if your child is **older than 17?** Or what if, as you read the descriptions of Indigo Children, you recognized not only your child, but you also recognized **yourself?**

You may be an Adult Indigo, whose spiritual woundings of childhood went unhealed, and were carried over to adulthood.

There is a spiritual healing process for your children older than seventeen, and for you, too!

This healing is called:

---

## The Point of Essence Process
### Pro-Claiming the Truth of Who You Are

---

## The Platinums

There is a special sub-category of Indigo: The Platinum Indigo Children and Adult Platinums. Their Indigo-anguish is almost constant.

For them, there are special, unique spiritual healings called "The Limitation Release" and "The Redemption Process."

## In Your Hands

Over the years, many, many families of Indigo Children and Adult Indigos have come to play the YOUMEES, *GraceLight,* and *The Point of Essence Process* and to experience healing. Many people have become trained Facilitators, taking these processes to their own parts of the world.

But there are millions of Indigo Children and their families (you included!), and it is high time that all Indigos and their families are able to find relief and healing.

So, if you have Indigo Children, you and your children are no longer alone.

If you are an Adult Indigo, you are no longer alone either.

We happily offer this book as a practical handbook for you to facilitate these spiritual healings.

You can facilitate *The 17* for your own Indigo Children.

You can facilitate *GraceLight* for your young Indigo Children.

You can facilitate *The Point of Essence Process* for yourself.

This book that you are holding in your hands is your guide into the world of spiritual healing for your children—and for you.

Your children—and you—do not have to live in emotional pain any longer.

With these simple, yet profound, processes, Indigos can come into the fullness of their Being, and affirm their vision of perfection for our world.

## About This Book

Let us tell you a little about the book, and the amazing work you are about to be a part of.

The book is divided into three major parts.

The **first section** is for your Indigo Children between the ages of seven and seventeen. There, you will find the essay, "Trailing Clouds of Glory," which describes our understanding of the identity, definitions, and characteristics of Indigos, and the principles of spiritual development and healing. **We invite you to read this essay before playing with any of the games in the book, since it provides basic foundational information for all three processes.**

Following "Trailing Clouds of Glory," you will find the entire *17* process—how to play the 17 YOUMEE games, and how to "lock in" the healings to make them permanent.

The **second section** of the book is for your Indigo Children from birth to age seven. It begins with the essay "To Gaze With Undimmed Eyes." Following the essay, you will find complete instructions to facilitate *GraceLight* for your little Indigo, including the centerpiece of the process— the powerful "Weaving the Harmony."

The **third section** of the book is for Adult Indigos, those seventeen years of age and older. It begins with the essay "Who Am I?" and then takes you through *The Point of Essence Process*, which allows you to release all the Indigo woundings you have been carrying since childhood, so the full truth of the essence of your Being can begin to shine through.

## About the Healing

After reading all the material in this book, you may decide that you would like to work with a Certified Facilitator whom we trained at The Soul Center for Spiritual Healing, who knows how to gently and joyfully work with children and parents and how to clearly and effectively give the instructions for each process.

If you would like to find a Facilitator in your area, please look on our Website: www.soulbysoul.com, or call us at 1-877-SOUL-KID.

Yet you may be far from a Facilitator, or you may be most comfortable facilitating the processes by yourself.

This book, *Spiritually Healing the Indigo Children (and Adult Indigos, Too!)*, is your guide. It is a little bit like a good cookbook. Inside, you'll find "recipes"—**how-to, step-by-step instructions**—which will tell you everything you need to know about the principles of the three spiritual healings, and carefully, thoroughly, and with great honor and respect for your commitment to spiritual healing for your child and/or for yourself, takes you through the processes.

When you are doing *The 17* or *GraceLight* for your child, or *The Point of Essence Process* for yourself, it may be easier if you have a spouse or partner or friend help you conduct the healing session, because it can be difficult to serve as both participant and facilitator at the same time.

Yet if no one is available to help you, please feel enabled and empowered to do the sessions yourself.

As with any good recipe, it is important that you **follow the instructions as closely as possible,** so that you achieve the finest results. As you will learn, these processes are sacred ritual, which, to be most effective, must be done exactly. Yet do not worry if you do not understand the instructions fully, or if any instruction seems too complicated, or if you think you have made a mistake. Your own Spiritual Guides are with you. They, like you, want healing for your children and for you. So, they will guide and protect you through the process.

And all is as it should be.

Perhaps your child—or you—will get the full effect of the healing. Perhaps your child—or you—will get only partial effect of the healing. Either way, it will be exactly what your child—or you—need at this moment in time.

All is perfect.

## What to Expect

After reading all of this, you might suppose that playing with any of the Indigo spiritual healing processes will result in a complete reversal of (perceived) negative behaviors. In particular, some parents and teachers of Indigo Children hope that the healings will mean that children are easier to "manage" and "control"—that they will now behave in an "acceptable" manner.

These three spiritual healings do not "pour" our children into socially acceptable "molds." They are not a therapeutic alternative for the building of moral character, the teaching and modeling of ethical values, the constant involvement, continual care, and gentle discipline that show our children that we love them.

These three spiritual healings serve to soften—and, hopefully, remove—the pain and discomfort that Indigos feel in being who and what they are.

The healings make it possible for Indigos to live in this troubled and battered world without the constant suffering that comes from feeling different and isolated, and without the constant anguish that being in this Earth-life, separated from the Divine, evokes.

These healings are not designed to make Indigos "less" than they are, but to give them the newly-comfortable space and emotional freedom to be more and more of who they are.

These three spiritual healings are the avenues for Indigo Children and Adult Indigos to come into the fullness of their Indigo-ness. Indigos who have experienced one of these three spiritual healings will become wiser, *more* insightful, *more* energetic, *more* precocious than before. They will have less need and respect for rules and authority. They will have less tolerance for the mundane and the commonplace. They will not "suffer fools easily." *And* they will be able to share their vision of perfection, and articulate their wisdom, with greater ease and comfort, with less anger and reactivity, with more patience, and understanding, and greater sensitivity to the world around them. They will be more successful Indigos.

This reality may be uncomfortable for those who insist on holding on to the old forms and the old authoritarian structures. But this Indigo reality is very, very good for our evolving and transforming world.

**Remember: The Indigos have come to this Earth to envision and embody the coming perfection of our world. Earth's evolution depends on the amazing gifts these children bring.** And these three spiritual healings will open them to fulfill their mission.

We—and our world with us—will be enriched by celebrating the fullness of their Indigo Beings, embracing them fully in their Indigo task, and following them to the fulfillment of their Indigo vision.

## Embracing the Blessing

Our children—and we—are precious spiritual Beings—unique in all the world. There is no reason for our children—or for us—to be in spiritual pain any longer.

Our children—and we—can now lay claim to our Divine gifts, and come into the fullness of our Being, embrace the greatness of our soul-mission, and hold steady our vision of perfection.

The world needs us, and what we have to give.

The world is waiting.

And as the ancient sage so keenly reminds us, the time is now.

The disciples informed the master
that the neighboring forest had burned to the ground.
The master said, "We must replant all the cedar trees."
The disciples said,
"But, Master, cedar trees take 2000 years to grow."
The master said,
"Then, there is not a minute to lose.
Come.
We must begin at once."

# The 17

## Spiritually Healing Children's Emotional Wounds

SPIRITUAL HEALING FOR INDIGO CHILDREN
AGES 7–17

# TRAILING CLOUDS
## OF
# GLORY

## We Believe

**We believe that children being born today are coming to Earth as pure channels of God.**

They come, in the words of the poet, "Not in entire forgetfulness. . . . But trailing clouds of glory . . . from God who is our home."

They are still basking in the glow of God's Light.

They are filled with God's Love.

Their old, old souls are still warm with the memory of eternal and universal knowledge.

Their deep, deep eyes hold the wisdom—and the secrets—from before the beginning of time until the end of days.

Most of all, they know the Divine blueprint for our universe. They come to Earth holding a clear and immediate vision of peace and perfection for us and for our world.

Yet "the rules" of living in this Earth-world make it impossible for our children to retain their complete knowing. If every person on Earth had universal knowing, then Earth would be a perfect place, a place just like Paradise. That, of course, is the ultimate goal for our world. But Earth is not yet Eden.

*So, an old legend teaches that, in the High Heavens, all souls are close to God, and spend their time learning all the secrets of the universe.*

*But when a soul comes to Earth, it cannot bring all its knowing. So, just as a soul—now in a body—is to be born, an angel taps the baby on the upper lip, leaving that little indentation right under its nose.*

*With this gentle touch, the soul forgets all the knowledge and the secrets of the whole universe, and keeps just enough wisdom and understanding to be a Human Being on Earth.*

Until they are four or five or six years old, our children, fresh from the Other Side, continue to reflect Divine Light, and hold onto some of the knowing and the secrets.

A story, which some claim is true, and others insist is an "urban legend":

*When a newborn was brought home, his older brother asked to be alone with the baby. The parents were puzzled by the request, but they granted their older son's wish. Standing near the crib, the older brother was heard to whisper, "Quick, baby. Tell me the secrets that I'm supposed to remember but that I'm already forgetting."*

Perhaps the story is just a myth, but here is an account that I know is true, because I was there as witness.

*Four-year-old Joey was in preschool, and had become "best friends" with William. Joey's parents thought that William was a very nice boy, but they were surprised that Joey felt so close to him; they thought that there were a number of other children in the class with whom Joey would have more in common. So, I asked Joey a simple question, "Did you know William from before?" "Sure," he replied. "When?" I asked. Joey pointed his thumb straight upward and, matter-of-factly said, "When we were with God."*

More and more of us are becoming aware that the lens through which our children see and perceive is open wider than ever before.

Yet it is not just these parental reports that confirm our children's knowing and remembering. Now, scientific research is affirming what these stories tell.

A recent study holds that babies have perfect musical pitch when they are born. But, according to the researcher, "the ability goes away because it serves no useful purpose in day-to-day life." We can only begin to imagine what other many perfections our children bring to this Earth-life that "go away" because they "serve no useful purpose." Sadly, the limitations and realities of Earth-life drain our children's knowing and diminish their perfection.

If they are asked at the right time and in the right way, sometimes, our children will remember and tell of the Other Side.

But, slowly, they forget.

Day-by-day, year-by-year, they lose their eternal soul-wisdom and soul-purity; their vision of perfection slowly dims, and they become "citizens-of-the-Earth-as-it-is-now." Much forgetting is according to plan.

Yet there is always a faint light in the shadows; the forgetting is never total. Every soul retains sparks of eternal knowledge, and, every now and then, everyone can get a "hit" or can see a glimpse or a glimmer of what we once knew, but have now forgotten. Some call it "intuition"; some call it "déjà vu"; some call it "extra sensory perception." We call it "soul memory."

---

## Parents!

From the moment your children are born, often say to them,
"Remember the secrets from the Other Side,
from when you were with God.
Then, when you get old enough to talk,
you can tell me what you remember."

You'll be doing your children, and yourself—and the
Universe—a great favor. The thinner and thinner the veil
between This Side and the Other Side becomes;
the more eternal knowledge we are able to grasp;
the more we know about the secrets of existence;
the closer and closer we will come to a world of perfection.
Our children will show us the way.
And we can help them to remember!

---

Because of—or, perhaps beyond—their inherent knowing and their vision of perfection, these children are often described as "highly intelligent," "extremely bright," "gifted," "quick," "precocious," "full of energy," "exceptionally talented," "incredibly creative," "wise beyond their years," and most often "get it" far more quickly than the adults around them.

They are highly self-reliant and self-sufficient, and they usually have very high self-esteem.

They are said to possess an almost "royal" sense of entitlement.

They are not comfortable with "old forms." They have little tolerance for "rules that make no sense," and little patience for people who don't "get it" as quickly and thoroughly as they do.

As a result, they hold little regard for societal norms, and have little respect for authority. They rarely meet preconceived expectations. They can often be quite demanding, and are often seen as nonconformist and, even, antisocial.

Clearly, they fit into no predetermined "mold."

In their pathfinding books,[1] Lee Carroll and Jan Tober call these knowing children (using a designation first made by Nancy Ann Tappe) "The Indigo Children," after a deep blue light that is sometimes seen enveloping them.

We call them "Children of Spirit."

We sense that fifty years ago, some 5 percent–10 percent of the children coming to Earth were "Indigos."

**We believe that now, more than 80 percent of all newborns are "Indigos,"** giving our world an extraordinary and ever-growing circle of wise and wondrous souls.

## Away from Home

Even with—perhaps, because of—the Light and Love they bring, and even with the expansion and evolving consciousness they mean for our world, our children have a big problem.

---

[1] Carroll, Lee and Jan Tober. *The Indigo Children: The New Kids Have Arrived.* Hay House, Inc., California, 1999.

———. *An Indigo Celebration: More Messages, Stories and Insights from the Indigo Children.* Hay House, Inc., California, 2001.

Increasingly, more and more of our children are having a terrible time living this Earth-life. **They come in perfection, and they are tossed into our wildly imperfect world.**

> *A mother decided that it was time to teach her seven-year-old son about "the facts of life," and tell him "where babies come from."*
>
> *So, the mother got all the age-appropriate books, and read them to her son. Gently—and beautifully—she explained about love and sex.*
>
> *As the crowning lesson, she got a videotape of an actual child-birth, and, together, mother and son watched the birthing.*
>
> *Viewing the tape, the young boy began to get more and more upset.*
>
> *Finally, quite concerned, he said to his mother, "That hurts a real lot, doesn't it?"*
>
> *"To be perfectly honest with you," she said, "yes it does. It hurts a great deal."*
>
> *The young boy thought for a long moment, and, then, very quietly, he asked, "And does it hurt the mother, too?"*

**On the "inside," children—who still retain some of the purity of having recently been with God—intuitively know what is right and good.** These children well remember the gentle, sweet love of the Other Side, and they hold within themselves a vision of a perfected world, an eternal knowing of what our world can be.

Yet the children see and experience this world—the "outside" with all that is wrong and evil—and feel the stark differences. They hear of warfare, abject poverty, debilitating hunger, rampant disease. They learn of murder and mayhem, hatred and bigotry. They know that their own schools and playgrounds have become killing fields. They experience injustice and inhumanity. They see the damage of drugs and drink. They feel the darkness that so often envelops our world.

When our children experience this great chasm between the perfection and holiness of their source, and the battered bruised existence they find here, they feel wounded at the core of their spiritual, energetic Beings. Their hearts and their souls ache.

When they feel a huge gap between what they intuitively forever-know from the Divine, and what they encounter here in Earth-experience, they become like shattered vessels, unable to hold holy Light, unable to sustain holy Energy.

> The tremendous dissonance
> between their perfect knowing
> and their greatly imperfect this-world experience
> causes our children
> great pain and anguish.
>
> For most adults, life's greatest pain and loneliness comes
> when, through our own actions or our own thoughts,
> we somehow disconnect and are separated from God.
>
> For our children, life's greatest pain, angst,
> and existential loneliness comes because,
> even though they desperately want
> to stay connected to God,
> the discordant forces of Earth-life cause shattering,
> and bring about separation.

In their pain, so many of our children are angry, and sad, and in despair. They feel so uncomfortable in their bodies; they are disillusioned, and confused, and uncertain. They have a very hard time coping with life. So, in their fear and desperation, our children "play out," and "act out" their pain. Many of our children lash out in ways that are deeply harmful to themselves and to those around them.

That is why, these days, we get reports about three, four, five, six-year old children—innocent babies—who sadly yet adamantly tell their parents, "I don't belong here. I don't want to be here. I want to go home. I want to be dead."

Our children experience additional emotional woundings here on Earth. As much as we want to care for them and protect them, no child lives in a totally safe cocoon. No child is free from hurt. Every child experiences emotional woundings that come as a natural part of childhood.

Now and then, a sorely misguided person will purposely try to injure a child. But most often, children are unwittingly wounded.

Parents, caretakers, teachers, coaches, playmates—anyone and everyone—can say and do things which wound a child's emotional body, and cause bewilderment, confusion, and pain. Because of their heightened awareness and sensitivities, so many of our children are now much more susceptible to feeling the effects and the consequences of these emotional wounds.

# And So

Because we, their parents and teachers, often think in "traditional" terms, and because we are not always aware of the uniqueness of these special children and the pain they are experiencing, we often consider these young ones "difficult children," who are "hard to manage and hard to control," who "act out," and are unable to "fit in."

They are accused of not "getting along" with parents, siblings, teachers, friends. They are called "troublemakers," and they are blamed for provoking turmoil at home and at school. They may be looked upon as "unhappy," "angry," "depressed." They are often given labels: "learning disabled"; "hyper-active"; "attention-deficient."

The children themselves are confused and bewildered. Why, they wonder, don't people understand? Why are we considered "strange" and "different" when it is really the rest of the world that is so out of tune with the harmonies of creation?

Sadly, many parents and teachers do not know how "to handle them," how to "cope with them." So, they are often put in special education classes, shuttled from counselor to therapist, and medicated with drugs.

For, when all else has failed, in our sincere—and often desperate—attempts to help our children, we have turned to medication. Sometimes drugs work. They can be successful in altering the brain chemistry just enough to ease our children's emotional pain and change their negative behavior. But, far too often, we are left with children who are "drug-managed" yet are still in pain and turmoil.

Yet despite the difficulties that our children have in living on this Earth, and despite the difficulties that parents and teachers—and society—have in coping with these children, we know that they are very special Human Beings.

**They are God's gift to ever-expanding world consciousness.**

They have a keen sense of purpose and destiny.

**They hold within themselves a vision of a perfected world, and they have come to show us the way.**

These precious children are "old souls," with eternal soul memory, who have come to open the way for a massive paradigm shift for our entire universe.

> OUR INDIGO CHILDREN
> ARE MAGNIFICENT BEINGS
> OF LIGHT AND LOVE.
>
> The difficulties they are having are not their fault!
> They are not to blame!
>
> From the place of their perfect knowing
> and their vision of perfection,
> they are merely reacting and responding to this troubled,
> battered, imperfect Earth-world in which they—and we—now live.
>
> It is we, their parents and teachers, who must understand
> the source and the depth of their pain,
> and who must find the ways to help our children
> feel safe and comfortable on this Earth.

## THE ATTEMPTS TO HEAL

Contemporary society has made numerous attempts to understand why our children are hurting and seeks myriad ways to help them heal. The government, the schools, the religious institutions, and the non-profit social service organizations have all devised hundreds and thousands of programs to help our children be healthy and whole—physically, intellectually, emotionally, and spiritually.

Their work is based on the theoretical and practical teachings of child development experts and educators, doctors and nurses, psychiatrists and psychologists, social workers and therapists, coaches and artisans, thinkers and writers, and, of course, parents and caretakers—anyone and everyone who cares about children. Their work is being bolstered by the ever-evolving data about how children grow and learn, and the continually new-found information about how DNA and genetic makeup affect children's behavior. Specifically, in the rearing of Indigo Children, Dr. Doreen Virtue[2] has taught how nutrition, supplements, environment, exercise, creativity, schooling, and advocacy can affect mood, attitudes, and behavior.

The myriad attempts to heal our children are good and worthy and valid. Most everyone who has tried to ease the pain of the Indigo Children has succeeded to some extent. Many have had significant impact.

But, collectively, all have failed.

## A New Approach to Healing

**The problem with all the current attempts to heal our children is that they have most all been made on a rational, intellectual, cognitive level.**

Yet the hurt and pain our children feel reside on the spiritual, energetic level.

Therefore, the healings must take place on that spiritual, energetic level.

## The World of Spirit

There is much beyond what we Human Beings know, and think, and feel, and see, and hear, and touch, and taste, and smell, and experience here in our Earth-world existence.

On the simplest level, for example, a dog hears the sound of a whistle that is inaudible to the human ear. The human sense of hearing is not developed enough to hear the highly pitched sound. Yet, surely, the sound exists. An AM radio does not have the capacity to receive FM signals. Yet, surely, the FM signals exist. A camera captures a picture that the lens is open wide enough to see. The camera does not have the capability to see anything outside the lens. Yet, surely, much more exists.

---

[2] Virtue, Doreen., Ph.D. *The Care and Feeding of Indigo Children.* Hay House, Inc., California, 2001.

The basic teaching from the World of Spirit is that everything—everything—of the cosmos was put in place at the moment of creation.

The whole of existence is already created.

It is waiting for Human Beings to develop enough, to imagine enough, to reach high enough, to discover it.

How do we find what is already there, but seems to be hidden from us?

We enter into the World of Spirit.

We give ourselves to knowing beyond what we know; seeing beyond what we see; hearing beyond what we hear; experiencing beyond what we experience.

We open ourselves to:

God

Source

Divine Energy

The Universe

Guidance

—call It/Him/Her what you will.

Like the biblical prophets, we open ourselves to intuition, night dreams, daydreams, visions, prayer, meditation, chant, body movement, channeling, soul memory.

We each embrace whatever method works best for us to receive and hold, if only for a few moments, the universal, eternal knowledge we once fully had, and will, eventually, have again—the very same knowing from the Other Side that our Indigo Children are holding for longer and longer.

The World of Spirit makes us aware of all the levels of existence beyond our current Earthly capabilities of access.

The World of Spirit is our gateway to evolving human consciousness, to the opening of our hearts and souls.

It brings us into the Divine presence.

It teaches us that there is really no separation between us and God, between us and all other Human Beings, between us and all existence.

It teaches us of the Wholeness, the Oneness, of the universe.

It teaches us that All is One. One is All. All is Love. Love is All.

> True consciousness
> —real enlightenment—
> is the knowing
> that there is actually never separation;
> there is only Oneness
> with Spirit,
> with God, and with the universe.

**The World of Spirit—through our Spiritual Guidance—has given us spiritual healing processes for our Indigo Children's emotional wounds.** And we have been given the mandate—and the joyous privilege—to give them over to the world.

We offer them to you with the most sincere and heartfelt hope and promise that our Indigo Children and Adult Indigos can be healed from the pain and anguish of their spiritual woundings.

## HEALING THE EMOTIONAL WOUNDINGS

**Remember: the emotional woundings our children feel are sourced in the sharp variance the child experiences between:** the "inside"—that which the child intuitively knows, and the "outside"—that which the child experiences in this world.

Since the children who are presently being born into this Earth-life are more fully immersed in God-Energy, and are more reflective of God-Light than any generation before them, and since they are at a higher soul—or "vibrational"—level than ever before, they, therefore, feel the dissonance between the "inside" and the "outside" more acutely than any previous generation of children.

Sometimes, the child is able to "bridge the gap" between "inside" and "outside," and can understand and control the emotional pain being experienced. At other times, the child cannot "bridge the gap," and either expresses the emotion in negative attitudes or behavior, or represses the emotion and "gets stuck" in it. Sometimes, a child cannot "bridge the gap," and cannot tolerate "being stuck" in the emotion or in its behavior. It is then that a child abandons his/her soul by engaging in conscience-less behavior, or by going mad, or by committing suicide.

To be emotionally healthy, the child has to release the emotional wounding. When the child is able to release the emotional wound, the child is, then, healed from that wound, and the dynamic of life is changed. Yet a child cannot just decide to "let go." Since the wounding is on the spiritual level, it can neither be identified cognitively nor healed through intellect.

Thus, the spiritual, energetic approach to healing emotional woundings is the healing of spirit.

## CHILDREN'S SPIRITUAL DEVELOPMENT

It is important to understand the nature of children's spiritual development, so that we can best comprehend their spiritual angst and anguish and best make available to them the most effective spiritual healings.

All Human Beings—especially young children—are deeply spiritual Beings. **Our Indigo Children on this Earth are "advanced" spiritual Beings, because of their longer continuing connection to God and the Other Side.**

Every child comes to this Earth with at least two Spiritual Guides. These Spiritual Guides sometimes manifest—that is, our children tell us about them—as Imaginary Friends or Imaginary Playmates. They are here to orient children to life on Earth, to support them through the adapting process.

The main task of these Guides is to keep our children connected, for as long as possible, to the Other Side to help them remember the secrets, to keep their vision of perfection always before them.

Even with their own Guides, young children are also under the "protection" of their parents' Guidance Teams. Since they are energetically connected to their parents through the parents' Guidance Teams, before the age of seven, children cannot act on their own to bring about their own spiritual healing. For, in order to actively participate in a spiritual healing process that requires active involvement, a child must be developmentally ready—both cognitively and spiritually.

A child must:

1) Have the cognitive, intellectual ability to understand, and act for him/herself on a rational level; and

2) Be an independent, self-sufficient spiritual Being; able to act for him/herself on an energetic level.

Children under the age of seven have not yet developed the cognitive abilities and skills to meaningfully participate in a healing session, and they are still connected to their parents by a "spiritual umbilical cord," and do not have the spiritual independence to act for themselves in bringing about healing. **So, for the spiritual healing of our Indigo Children from birth to age seven, the parent must "act for," or surrogate for, the child in the healing process.**

---

Spiritual woundings carried by
children from birth to age seven
are healed through the process called

GRACELIGHT
Weaving Harmony for the Littlest Indigos

described in the second section of this book.

---

**Somewhere around age seven**—as children become more connected to the everyday world around them—their Guides begin to fade from children's consciousness. That is why seven and eight-year-old children rarely talk about their Imaginary Friends anymore. That is also why seven and eight-year-old children often stop talking about the Other Side and about being with God.

**From approximately age seven, until they reach approximately age seventeen,** children's own Guides remain with them, but the Guides fade into the background and take less consciously active roles. These growing children are now solidly under their parents' Guidance Teams. Firmly ensconced under their parents' Guidance Teams—and cognitively developing—children from the ages of seven until seventeen can actively participate with their parent(s) in spiritual healing and be energetically healed.

For children ages 7 until 17, this healing process is:

---

# The 17

## Spiritually Healing Children's Emotional Wounds

a therapeutic process—sourced in the world of the Spirit—
that celebrates our children's inherent knowing;
heals their emotional woundings;
brings life-changing transformation to their attitudes and behaviors;
and affirms their soul-vision of a perfect world.

---

**Upon reaching the age of seventeen, a child no longer comes under the parents' Guidance Teams. At age seventeen,** a person's own extended Guidance Team can begin to form—led by the Guides who have been there all along and who now come to the fore again. That is why someone over the age of seventeen can no longer be spiritually healed through *The 17* process, but must be energetically responsible for his/her own healing.

---

Spiritual woundings carried by
Adult Indigos
are healed through

## The Point of Essence Process

Pro-Claiming the Truth of Who You Are

described in the third section of this book.

---

For those who come to Earth with a contract for a specific soul mission, the MasterGuides who will assist with that soul mission appear when it is time for the mission to unfold.

The formation of the Guidance Team can be a slow, deliberate process, and can depend on many factors.

Interestingly, and, often, most painfully, the period when a Guidance Team is forming but is not yet fully formed—most typically when a young person is between the ages of 17 and 25—is the time when a young person is most vulnerable and at risk for mental and emotional imbalance, including the emergence of dis-eases such as schizophrenia and bi-polar disorder. The lack of solid Spiritual Guidance can be a major determining factor that leads to confusion, despair, and, even possibly, a break with reality.

The ability to successfully live in contentment and satisfaction—and, yes, even to live at all—on this Earth can well depend on spiritual healing. That is why it is so important for Indigo Children who carry the emotional woundings of childhood to be spiritually healed through *GraceLight* or *The 17*, and for those seventeen years of age or older, our Adult Indigos, to be healed through *The Point of Essence Process.*

# THE 17

# HOW IT WORKS

## THE WOUNDINGS

**We have identified 17 emotional wounds that Indigo Children can hold.**

These woundings have this-world names, but because these woundings are on the spiritual, energetic level, they are defined differently from the way they would be known on the rational, cognitive level.

> Each wounding is sourced in the separation from God,
> and the bewilderment and pain that results.

As we explore these wounds individually, we will see how children behave when they have been touched by each one.

As well, each of these emotional wounds is centered in a unique place in the physical body. As we explore each of these wounds individually, we will see just how each emotional wound affects the specific place in the physical body where it resides.

The woundings, their definitions, and where they are centered in the body:

# 1. ANGER

The need to defend oneself, through attack,
against the harshness of this-world experience.

CENTERED IN:
**THE RIGHT PALM**

# 2. GRIEF

Weeping at the separation.

CENTERED IN:
**THE THROAT**

# 3. FEAR

The experience of being in danger because
of being too small, "too little."

CENTERED IN:
**THE KIDNEYS**

# 4. DISTRUST

Not being able to count on any reality as certain.

CENTERED IN:
**THE BACK OF THE KNEES**

# 5. DESPAIR

Giving up the connection to the breath of God.

### CENTERED IN:
**THE HEART**

# 6. ANGUISH

The belief in aloneness.

### CENTERED IN:
**THE LOWER INTESTINES**

# 7. SHAME

Being embarrassed in front of the whole cosmos.

### CENTERED IN:
**THE INNER LEFT EAR**

# 8. INSECURITY

The experience of having no solid ground inside.

### CENTERED IN:
**THE STOMACH**

# 9. SELFISHNESS

The fear of coming out to interact
with this-world experience.

CENTERED IN:
**THE BACK OF THE HEELS**

# 10. LOSS

Not being able to find one's own heart.

CENTERED IN:
**THE LUNGS**

# 11. PANIC

The experience of being suspended in mid-air
with nothing to grasp or hold on to.

CENTERED IN:
**THE ADRENALS**

# 12. INFERIORITY

The belief "I'll never be as good as God."

CENTERED IN:
**THE CHEST**

## 13. HATRED

The experience of feeling as though
one does not deserve reunion.

CENTERED IN:
**THE LIVER**

## 14. INDIGNATION

Holding righteousness in response to the lack
of dignity expressed for God's creatures.

CENTERED IN:
**THE RIGHT HIP**

## 15. RESENTMENT

The wish that the world matches the inner vision.

CENTERED IN:
**THE GALLBLADDER**

## 16. JEALOUSY

Wanting what the angels have.

CENTERED:
**BELOW THE EYES**

# 17. GUILT

Holding oneself responsible for the lack
of perfection in the world.

## CENTERED IN:
## THE RIGHT SHOULDER JOINT

Often, a child is aware of the wounding and cognizant of the pain. Just as often—probably more often—a child is unaware of the exact moment or incident of emotional wounding but still deeply feels the pain and hurt.

Once emotionally wounded, the child retains that wound until it is healed. Left unhealed, the wound's manifest behavior can lead to increasingly anti-social behavior. At their worst, the woundings and their manifest behavior lead children to not know the difference between right and wrong. At their very worst, the woundings and their manifest behavior lead to children without conscience—children who may steal for drug money and bring guns to school to shoot their classmates and teachers.

## UNBLOCKING THE WOUNDINGS

**When our children are emotionally wounded, their emotional flow— their channel of God-Light and God-Energy—becomes dense and, eventually, is blocked.** Their pain "pools" in particular emotional/physical areas of their Being and sources their negative behavior.

In order to transform negative behavior, we need to get to the source that is fueling the behavior. We need to find a way to unblock the clog, to drain the pool of pain, so that the channel can be open, so that Light and Energy easily flow, and negative behavior will cease.

Picture this: If we drain water from a car battery, the car cannot move. For, when its power source is drained of its "charge," it has no energy and cannot work.

In the same way: If we can "drain the energy" from a child's emotional wounding, if we can be sure that the wounding no longer has the power source-charge—if we can unclog the pool of pain—then:

The wound has no energy.
The child can heal.
The flow of Light and Energy is reestablished.
And the negative behavior will stop.


# The YOUMEES

The way to go to the source, to "drain the energy" of each separate wounding, is through playing a little ritual/ceremony/game designed especially for that particular wound. **There is one healing ritual/game for each of the 17 spiritual woundings.**

**The ritual/ceremony/game is to be played by the child and one parent.**

It does not matter which parent—either mother or father—plays the healing games with the child. And it does not matter which gender parent plays the games with which gender child—either mother or father can play the games with either son or daughter. If a biological parent is not available to play the healing games, the procedures work just as well with the primary caretaker of the child—blood-related or not.

**Each healing game is called a YOUMEE, because it is done between "you" and "me."**

Who is the "you" and who is "me"? The parent is both the "you" and the "me," and the child is both the "you" and the "me." The name YOUMEE implies the deep inter-connection between the child and the parent playing the healing game.

> The parent is not a healer, nor does the parent impose
> a particular healing on a child.
>
> Rather, the parent is a facilitator—a caring, loving helper—
> for healing and transformation that comes from
> the spirit and energy of God and the universe,
> that embraces—and is embraced by—a child's soul.

**Each YOUMEE takes no more than two or three minutes to play.**

**Each YOUMEE has a slightly different procedure for boys and for girls.** For example, a girl may start a game with her right hand, while a boy starts with his left hand. This is because there are "right brain"—"left brain" differences between males and females, which are also manifest on a spiritual, energetic level. The slight differences in procedures respond to this male-female difference.

## SACRED RITUAL

**Each YOUMEE is played by following a specific and an exact order of words and actions.** YOUMEES are like sacred rituals given to us from the World of Spirit. We know the power of words and rituals. Sacred rituals magnify the everyday; they open and enlarge our space and our perceptions; they link us to that which is greater than we; they bring Heaven to Earth; they bring comfort and blessing to our lives.

Every culture has magical words that carry great energy and power:

"Once upon a time."

"They lived happily ever after."

"Open sesame."

"Abracadabra."

"I pledge allegiance."

"Holy, Holy, Holy." (In the original Hebrew, "*Kadosh, Kadosh, Kadosh.*" In Latin, "*Sanctus, Sanctus, Sanctus.*")

We cannot say: "Holy, Holy, Bozo." By changing even one syllable of the ritualistic formula, we dilute the purpose and the power of the words.

In the same way, every culture has magical actions that carry great energetic power.

The Catholic crossing.

The Jewish Torah service.

The Japanese tea ceremony.

The flag-raising order.

The seventh inning stretch.

The religious rites of standing, sitting, bowing, kneeling in prayer.

We cannot cross ourselves in the wrong direction, or turn our backs to the Torah, or have one teacup out of place, or stand when we are supposed to kneel. By changing even one motion of the ritualistic formula, we dilute the purpose and the power of the actions.

It is the same with playing the YOUMEES.

Spiritual Guidance has given us the exact order, and the exact words, and the exact motions for each YOUMEE. To be effective—to work at all— the YOUMEES must be played exactly according to instructions, exactly according to the script that is given. By changing even one word or one motion of the YOUMEES, we dilute the purpose and the power of the ritual-games, and they will not work. They will not be effective energetic tools for healing.

So, please remember:

---

## PLAY EACH YOUMEE

# EXACTLY

## ACCORDING TO THE SPECIFIC INSTRUCTIONS

---

It may seem as if the YOUMEES are odd little games that have nothing to do with a particular wounding or a particular behavior. But remember: the healing is not taking place on a cognitive, intellectual level, which can be readily or rationally explained. **The healing is being done at a spiritual, energetic**

**level.** It is on this spiritual level that our Guidance—and our experience—shows us that the YOUMEES work and that healing takes place.

# Playing the YOUMEES

A YOUMEE healing session is played in an ordered sequence.

1.  Setting Sacred Space

2.  Performing the Energy Balance

3.  Doing the Illumination

    > This Illumination identifies which spiritual woundings a child is holding. These are the woundings that will be healed through the playing of the appropriate YOUMEES. Usually, when playing the YOUMEES for the first time, a child will be holding no more than nine woundings.

4.  Reciting the Intention

5.  Playing the YOUMEES

6.  Reciting the Seal of Gratitude

7.  Reciting The Limitation Release, if needed

8.  Anchoring in the Healing

The guide to playing the YOUMEES—which is the next section of this book—gives you step-by-step detailed instructions for facilitating a YOUMEE healing session with your child.

## COMPLETING THE HEALING

Three months after the first YOUMEE session, you and your child play the YOUMEES again.

This time, you play the YOUMEE games for ALL THE REMAINING WOUNDINGS—the woundings that were NOT Illuminated during the first session as present in your child. These remaining woundings are healed through the playing of their YOUMEES during the second session.

Thus, at the conclusion of the second session, the YOUMEES for all 17 spiritual woundings will have been played, and all the woundings will have been permanently spiritually healed.

What does it mean that playing the YOUMEES produces "permanent" healing? Will our Indigo Children be "cured" of their pain and anguish, never to experience suffering again? That, of course, would be ideal, but in this Earth-world that is not yet Paradise, a life without pain is still not possible.

So, to understand the "permanent" healing that playing the YOUMEES produces, envision a broken arm. The bone is broken into two or more pieces. The doctor immobilizes the bone and puts a cast on the arm. Over several weeks, the bone "knits" back together, and, eventually, the broken arm is repaired. A "protective shield" has been placed around the injury. The break is "permanently" healed.

In some cases, the place of the break will be stronger than ever before. In some cases, the place will be vulnerable—perhaps, even more susceptible—to future injury. In either case, there is no guarantee that the arm bone will not break again. A different accident or injury could result in another break.

It is the same with the 17 spiritual woundings that the YOUMEES heal. **These specific woundings—the ones the child holds from birth and acquires until the YOUMEES are played—are "permanently" healed through the two YOUMEE sessions. A "protective shield" is placed around them, and those specific woundings will not manifest again.**

Yet it is surely possible that a child can be "re-injured." The normal circumstances of everyday life may produce the settings and the situations where sensitive Indigo Children may be re-wounded. Having played the YOUMEES will make Indigo Children less susceptible to the possibility of new woundings, but will not eliminate the possibility altogether.

Before playing the YOUMEES, Indigo Children are "open windows" who take in all the hurts of Earth-life. Playing the YOUMEES "shuts" the window—"permanently." Yet sometimes—from the outside or the inside—the window is opened just a crack, or, sometimes, an unforeseen incident can shatter the pane of glass.

So, parents and Indigo Children—now highly attuned to the nature of spiritual woundings—will sense if a "shattering," the formation of new spiritual woundings, has occurred. Then, parents and Indigo Children—now highly aware of the power of YOUMEE healings—can tap into your own knowing to determine if and when a "BOOSTER" YOUMEE session will be helpful.

# The 17: It's Fun!

Even though *The 17* is a powerful and effective therapeutic technique, it is good to remember that the YOUMEES are designed as games—games for children and parents to joyfully play together. If a YOUMEE session is presented to children as therapy or healing, it may seem intimidating or frightening, or it may provoke anxiety and reluctance. But if the YOUMEE session is presented as a chance to play games and have fun, then children's anticipation and participation can be happy and enthusiastic.

The very best thing for parents and children to know and remember about *The 17* is: Playing the YOUMEES is fun!

Here are a few of the very positive feelings expressed by parents after playing the YOUMEE games with their children:

♦ "I felt safe and liked the playful atmosphere."

♦ "My son and I enjoyed this very much, and we both felt great afterward."

♦ "I truly enjoyed the games. They were very powerful for me in terms of seeing my son as a loving Human Being."

♦ "Some of the games elicited emotional responses in me as a parent."

♦ "Immediately after the session, she seemed very happy, saying that she really enjoyed doing the games with me, and that she knew that no matter what ever happens to us as a family, we will always love each other."

♦ "Afterwards, I felt closer to my child than ever before."

---

## THE YOUMEES ARE GAMES
## THAT ARE FUN TO PLAY!

---

# THE 17: IT WORKS!

We and our trained Facilitators have played the YOUMEES with hundreds and hundreds of children and their parents.

The measurement of results has not been subject to rigid scientific research standards. And it is, of course, possible that just the time that parents and children spend together and the intimate interaction between parents and children that playing the YOUMEES entails produce some good results.

Yet our anecdotal findings—the reports of parents about their children— are extremely positive. **Parents report swift, powerful, and profound change in children's behavior and attitudes soon after playing the YOUMEES.**

A few comments from parents playing the YOUMEE games:

♦ "Calmer and appears to be sleeping better . . . More independent."

♦ "Happier, calmer. Babysitter reports that she is more focused."

♦ "Less frustrated . . . Hasn't been as demanding . . . Enjoys his time with himself."

♦ "Less prone to angry outbursts . . . Calmer . . . More peaceful . . . Lighter in mood."

♦ "More cordial and engaging . . . More loving . . . Less anxious . . . More hugging . . . More conversational at mealtimes . . . Says he is enjoying church youth group more."

♦ "Calmer . . . Doesn't argue with me as much as before . . . More centered and less depressed . . . I am almost 100 percent sure that she is not using any drugs or alcohol."

♦ "More considerate of (brother's) feelings . . . Shares without being prompted . . . Has seemed more 'centered' to me."

♦ "Very much in balance with himself . . . Doing well on home-work . . . Communication is better . . ."

♦ "Seems to be more at peace with herself and others . . . Appears to be more relaxed."

♦ "More loving . . . Giving more hugs and kisses."

♦ "An overall growth in his sense of self and self-confidence."

♦ "In the last two weeks, he has had quite a few nights in a row without bed-wetting."

♦ "His well-being seems improved, and he is much more responsive to family needs."

♦ "His grandparents have noticed that he is much more relaxed in their company . . . He is less demanding and sweeter."

♦ "She seems more cooperative and less angry."

♦ "More focused . . . More self-sufficient . . . More helpful . . . I am grateful for the way both girls seem more settled and grounded."

♦ "More open. He gets along better with his brothers . . . More willing to uphold his responsibilities, i.e., math packets, piano practice, chores around the house. . . . Doesn't seem as adamant or stubborn."

♦ "(His) positive attitude makes the whole family more dynamic and positive."

♦ "Seems less dependent on mommy. This last month (she) has been quite happy and very social."

♦ "Grandma says (he) is more loving and smiles more. He has not been hurtful toward his friends."

♦ "Talking about feelings more than just getting angry and crying. . . . Less negativity about being asked to do something."

♦ "She appears to be more loving and accepting of others. She is more aware of feelings . . . She seems to be in a good place emotionally."

♦ "I feel he has been less stressed and more laid back. (During this past month), it has been a pleasure to be his mom!"

♦ "(She) used to fight with me all the time. Right now, she fights with me only 50 percent of the time, and the other time she behaves like an angel. . . . I have more peace with her. I trust her more. I think [almost sure] that she doesn't lie to me anymore."

♦ "Happier . . . More 'smiley.' Lighter in mood."

♦ "Glad we did this. I think that it has made us more gentle with one another."

One young man and his experience playing the YOUMEES serves as a prime example.

He was about twelve years old, and he was wearing long, baggy shorts, dirty sneakers, and a brightly colored 1960s-like psychedelic tie-dye T-shirt. On top of his head was the biggest mop of curly red hair I had ever seen. Even though he was scowling, I took an instant liking to him.

Then he opened his mouth. "I'm really pissed," he said, in a very, very angry voice. "I don't want to be here."

"Hi," I said. "Nice to meet you, too."

He scowled even more, and gave me one of those looks that said, "What kind of jerk are you?"

"So, tell me," I asked, "if you don't want to be here, then why are you here?"

"SHE made me come," he replied, pointing a very accusing finger at his mother—a lovely woman with short blond hair, dressed rather conservatively. "She made me come, and I don't want to be here."

"I understand," I said. "So tell me, why don't you want to be here?"

"First of all, it was a long drive."

I was rather surprised at that complaint, because I knew that they had come from only 45 minutes away, but time is relative, especially to an almost-teenage boy.

"Uh-humm," I murmured, not wanting to be very committal.

"But that's not the worst thing. The worst thing is that I have to be away from my computer."

"Away from your computer?" I asked. "Why is that such a bad thing?"

"You don't understand either!" he shouted. "You don't get it! You just don't get it! My whole life is in that computer! My SOUL is in that computer!"

"Wow," I thought to myself. What an amazing—and sad—thing for a twelve-year-old to say. His whole life is wrapped up in a machine? His whole Being identified with surfing the Net? His soul is in a computer?

And at the same time, I thought how incredibly perceptive and self-examined this young man is. How wonderful that, at his age, he can know, and define, and articulate himself so well.

I really didn't know what to say. After all, from his perspective, he had a very good point. So, I said the first thing that came to my mind. I said, "Maybe you should get a laptop."

"See, Mom," he said adamantly. "I told you. I told you. I need a laptop. That way I can have my computer everywhere."

The mother didn't look too pleased. It seemed as if her son had just recruited an ally—a grownup, no less—for what must have been his ongoing and probably rather insistent demand.

Immediately, I regretted my flippant words. I surely hadn't meant to pit parent against child, especially with a suggestion that might cost mom thousands of dollars.

Yet in the back of my mind, I couldn't help but think that getting a laptop might not be such a bad idea. After all, if his soul is in the computer, with a laptop, he will never have to abandon his soul. He can keep his soul with him wherever he goes.

He told us that "the only good thing" about himself is that he is an expert at downloading music onto his computer and that he had "cracked the code" to download certain Japanese computer games. He said that he doesn't have any real friends and that the only reason that "the guys" talk to him at school is because they want to take advantage of his skills with the computer. He told us that he spends all his time in his room listening to music and playing computer games. Even though he lives in a beach community, he told us that he doesn't like to be outside, he is afraid of water, and he never goes swimming. His only "claim to fame" is that he had sent away for a BB gun from a mail-order company, and he had "shot up the neighborhood" before his mother—SHE—found out and confiscated the gun.

About three weeks after we played the YOUMEES with him, his mother called to tell us that there seemed to be a complete turnaround in her son. He now spends a couple of afternoons a week shooting baskets at the school playground. One of the boys from his class in school called to invite our friend to join his family in a spring break cruise to Mexico—and he, who is afraid of water, and would have to leave his computer at home, readily accepted.

Last weekend, mother and son visited with her parents, and he—who usually sat sullen and silent at these family gatherings—had engaged his grandfather in an animated conversation. And a couple of nights ago, our young friend looked at his mother and said, "You know, those YOUMEE people weren't so bad. They must be doing something right."

Over and over again, we heard the same report: When children play the YOUMEES, their emotional pain and spiritual angst seem to diminish, and their lives seem more comfortable and happy.

## The Platinum Indigos

There is a sub-category of Indigo Children who need a more powerful spiritual healing than even *The 17* can provide. These are the Platinum Indigos, born beginning in 1964.

**Some 60 percent of the Indigo Children now on Earth are Platinum Indigos.**

**A Platinum Indigo comes into this Earth-life carrying a cellular imprint from his/her most recent previous lifetime.**

For these Platinum Indigos, the most recent previous lifetimes came to an end in the 1960s and the 1970s when the bodies they inhabited died in a drug-induced daze or a coma, or in combat in Vietnam (where drug use was prevalent).

Guidance teaches that our most recent previous incarnation can have a very profound impact in this incarnation. We carry strong cellular memory from our last lifetime, which can affect us even on a physiological level in this lifetime. So, someone who died filled with drugs, or who died in brutal combat, is very likely to bring vestiges of those experiences into this lifetime, and display characteristics that reflect those experiences.

For Platinum Indigos, this cellular imprint affects the neural pathways in the brain, manifesting in the nervous system easily "short-circuiting." As a result, these children display a marked hypersensitivity to things like noise, intensity of emotion, confusion and chaos, challenging situations.

They can be highly allergic to certain foods and environmental conditions.

They have a very low tolerance for frustration and stress.

Their parents often tell of them "losing it" or having "melt-downs."

They often have learning disorders and/or comprehension and expression disorders.

Playing the YOUMEES is effective for these children's "regular" Indigo spiritual woundings, but it is not a healing-response to the behaviors that arise from being a Platinum Indigo.

The Platinums are Carrying a Memory Impact, which requires an additional spiritual healing. This healing is called The Limitation Release and is recited by the child near the end of a YOUMEE session.

If you sense that your child is a Platinum Indigo Carrying a Memory Impact, who would benefit from this special healing, add The Limitation Release to your YOUMEE session immediately following the recitation of The Seal.

We believe that The Limitation Release, coupled with *The 17*, will soften the overt symptoms and help bring the deeper healing relief that your Platinum Indigo needs.

## The Nature of Healing

*The 17* healings will not work for every child; *The 17* is not necessary for every child. Only some 80 percent of the children being born now are Indigos. That means that 20 percent of our children will not behave as Indigos, will not feel the dissonance between this Earth and the Other Side that Indigos feel, and will not be as vulnerable or as sensitive to the energetic, emotional woundings sustained in this lifetime.

These children will most probably not need the deep spiritual healings that *The 17* provides, and if the YOUMEES are played, will, most likely, not respond in any significant way.

**Of the 80 percent of the children for whom *The 17* healings is appropriate, some may not respond in any affecting fashion.** But that is the nature of any and all healing therapies administered to individual, unique, free-will Human Beings. For myriad reasons—some known, some an enduring mystery—sometimes a healing process works; sometimes it does not.

Yet sometimes, a slight impediment to healing is present in the child, or in the parent-child relationship, or in the universe. Many of these impediments can be easily eliminated by "fine-tuning" *The 17* process.

If playing the YOUMEES seems to have not been effective, check the Fine-Tuning section of this book for suggestions as to what the impediment might be, and the simple ways to ease the impediment and bring about the healing.

Still we believe that for the vast majority of the Indigo Children who currently populate our earth, *The 17* can produce dramatic and effective life-change. *The 17* can be a formidable and powerful way to spiritually heal our children's energetic, emotional woundings.

## At Stake: Sky Blue

**Our children are the foundation of our world; on them, the world stands.** For only when our children's emotional wounds are healed can our world move to a higher dimension, to a higher soul—"vibrational"—level.

Moving to that higher dimension will mean that we will all have greater wisdom and understanding; that we can know beyond knowing and see beyond seeing; that our senses will be keener; that our consciousness will be more highly evolved; that we will all be more fully immersed in God-Energy and more reflective of God-Light.

Then—and only then—can our world move beyond the limitations of the present time into a time and place where universal healing can take place, where the hope and promise of a perfect world can become reality.

That perfect world is envisioned as a place where, hand in hand, parents and children lead us away from hatred and bigotry, warfare and violence, toward a time of reconciliation and healing, transformation and transcendence; a time of decency and dignity; justice and compassion; goodwill and gladness; harmony, peace, and love.

From a childhood game, we call the vision of that world, "Sky Blue."

Why "Sky Blue?" Do you remember playing hopscotch when you were young? With chalk, you draw a formation of numbered boxes on the sidewalk. The object of the game is to "hop" up those boxes and reach the very top—which some people call "#10," some people call "home," and some people call "goal." For some unknown reason, in Chicago, when we were growing up, we called that ultimate box **"Sky Blue."**

**"Sky Blue" is the very best place you can be—the pinnacle of perfection.**

The only way to reach Sky Blue is to invite our children—one by one; soul by precious soul—into healing, so that our world can move dimensions and reach toward that best-of-all-moments when joyful tranquility will envelop the universe, when there will be peace in every home and love in every heart.

Everything, everything, depends on how we act here and now.

With *The 17*, we now have the understanding; we now have the tools.

Now is the time to invite our children to healing, to invite them to embrace the fullness of their Beings.

Now is the time to journey toward Sky Blue.

## DEAREST PARENTS

As the shepherds and stewards of these remarkable soul-children, you face a great challenge and a rare opportunity. It used to be that a parent's main task was formation—guiding growth and development; teaching ethical values, moral right, and good character.

Now, being a parent means having an even greater and more awesome role—guiding our children toward transformation. Even though many of our children, because of their inherent knowing and all their Light, may perceive and be aware of much more about themselves than we, their parents, grasp, our singular and sacred job is to help sustain the Divine Light that is within our children.

Your children need you; they are counting on you. In the words of the ancient sage, Philo: "What God is to the world, parents are to their children." **The only way your children—and our world with them—can heal is when you make the conscious decision to be their hope, their guide.**

As you choose to lead them on their journey toward wholeness, we invite you to remember this story about the wise old sage who was once asked what the most satisfying experience had been in his long and illustrious life.

He thought for quite a while, and then he replied:

> I chanced to meet one day two small children—
> a young girl and her little brother—who were crying.
> A short conversation with the children revealed that they were lost.
> To the best of my ability, I tried to show them the way.
> Whereupon they went down the road singing.

May it be this way for you and your children.
And for our world with you.

# THE GUIDE
## TO
# PLAYING THE YOUMEES

## GETTING READY

1. To play the YOUMEES with your child, it will be easiest if you
   have a spouse or partner or friend help you conduct the healing session, because it can be difficult to serve as both parent
   and facilitator at the same time.

   Yet if no one else is available to help you, please feel
   enabled and empowered to do the sessions by yourself.

2. When you play the YOUMEES with your child at home, please
   consider your session to be a "scheduled appointment."

   Don't be interrupted by ringing telephones or
   doorbells.

   Don't be distracted by your other children.

   It is best that you make arrangements for
   your other children to be out of the house,
   or to be cared for by another, while you are
   playing the YOUMEES.

   In this way, you will not be distracted by
   worrying about your other children's
   whereabouts or well-being, their behavior
   or energy will not enter into the session,
   and your child with whom you are playing

the YOUMEES will not be concerned
with the attitudes or reactions of his/her
brothers/sisters.

3.  If you have more than one child with whom you want to play
    the YOUMEES, it may be tempting to schedule the sessions
    one right after the other, especially since the space is already
    set, and you are in the healing mood and mode.

    Yet we have found that sessions that are held one
    after another tend to hold less success for healing.

    Perhaps your energy is slightly lower in the
    second session.

    Perhaps some small percentage of your ener-
    gy and/or attention becomes focused away
    from the second session.

    Perhaps something in the house, or another
    child's whereabouts or well-being, causes
    some slight distraction.

    Whatever the reason that back-to-back sessions are not as
    effective as individual sessions, we suggest that it is best to
    separate the YOUMEE sessions for your two or more children
    by a number of hours, or, better yet, to hold the sessions on
    different days.

4.  It is best if the room in which you play the YOUMEES is light
    and airy.

    The room needs an empty area (free of furniture)
    large enough for playing the YOUMEES that require
    movement.

5.  To play the YOUMEES, you will need two chairs, such as fold-
    ing chairs or kitchen chairs, most preferably without arms,
    that can be easily moved.

    You will also need:
    two pieces of paper,
    a pen or pencil,
    and a pair of scissors.

# Playing the YOUMEES

1. Please familiarize yourself with the whole YOUMEE process by reading the entire set of instructions before you begin a YOUMEE session with your child.

2. Please follow the processes and the "script," according to instructions, as closely as you can.

   BEGIN BY:
   > Setting Sacred Space
   > Performing the Energy Balance
   > Doing the Illumination
   > Reciting the Intention

   THEN:
   > Play each YOUMEE step-by-step, following the numbered instructions.

   TO CONCLUDE THE SESSION:
   > Recite the Seal of Gratitude

   IF:
   > You sense that your child is a Platinum Indigo who is Carrying a Memory Impact,
   > Recite The Limitation Release

   THEN:
   > Recite the Anchor
   > Close the Sacred Space

3. When you complete the session, give your child a "gift" of a stone, or a seashell, or a little piece of driftwood—anything that comes directly from the natural world.

   > The energy of the Earth-element will support your child's integration of the healing, allowing the healing to be smoother and easier. As well, your child will cherish the little gift as a pleasant reminder of the sweet time spent with you playing the YOUMEES.

4.  Keep the Check-List on which you marked the YOUMEES that you played today. In this way, you will know which YOUMEES are left to be played in three months.

5.  Mark your calendar. Make an appointment with yourself for three months from now, when you will do the second session, playing all the YOUMEES with your child that you did not play in this first session.

    When you and your child have completed the second session, all the spiritual woundings will be healed, and the healings will be permanent.

---

As you embrace this sacred task,
we thank you and we honor you
for bringing spiritual healing
to your child.

---

# I
# SETTING SACRED SPACE

BEGIN BY SETTING THE PHYSICAL SPACE: The room in which the YOUMEES are played should be light and airy with an empty area (free of furniture) large enough for playing the YOUMEES that require movement.

HAVE: two folding chairs, two pieces of paper, a pen or pencil, and a pair of scissors.

NOW: For the playing of the YOUMEES to be most effective, set SACRED SPACE.

SETTING SACRED SPACE aligns the energy in the room with the Earth's Energy, invites in Divine Light, infuses the space with a vortex of Light Energy, and raises the space to a higher vibrational level.

This is best accomplished by symbolically representing Four Elements.

To do this, place symbols in the room—one in each of the four corners of the room—representing Earth's Four Elements. (It does not matter which symbol is in which corner of the room.)

1. A small bowl filled with dirt, or a piece of wood, or a rock, or a crystal, which represents the element of **Earth.**

2. A feather, or a filled balloon, which represents the element of **Air.**

3. A lamp, or a flashlight, with the lightbulb turned on, or a lighted candle, which represents the element of **Fire.**

4. A glass of water, which represents the element of **Water.**

After you have completed playing the YOUMEES,
please remember to close the Sacred Space
by removing the Earth Element symbols
from the room.

Continue with the ENERGY BALANCE.

# 2

# ENERGY BALANCE

In order to participate in this healing process, PARENT and CHILD must first balance your bodies, minds, emotional, and spiritual energies with the Earth's Energy.

Follow these simple steps to do the **ENERGY BALANCE.**

PARENT and CHILD:

1.  Sit on chairs, facing one another.

2.  Plant your feet firmly on the ground.

3.  Breathe deeply, inhaling and exhaling three times.

4.  Cross your arms over your chest, hands at your shoulders. Breathe deeply three times.

5.  Reverse your cross. Breathe deeply three times.

6.  PARENT and CHILD each touch his/her wrists together (as though hands are in a praying position) and spread hands apart slightly (as though hands are in a catching position).

And together, PARENT and CHILD say:

## *Love and Light*

Go on to the ILLUMINATION.

# 3

# ILLUMINATION

This is the way to determine which of the seventeen wounds your CHILD needs to heal at the first YOUMEE session.

1.  PARENT and CHILD continue sitting on chairs facing each other.

2.  PARENT: Take 30 to 60 seconds to "Tune into your child."

    Sit and look at your child sitting across from you.

    Let your heart to focus on your child,
    and try to get in touch with your child's feelings.

3.  PARENT say: "It is my intention that my heart be tuned into my CHILD's heart."

4.  PARENT: Take a pen or pencil and a piece of paper, and make a list of numbers from 1–17 on the paper.

    The list on the paper—which becomes the "Check-List"—will look like this:

1.
2.
3.
4.
5.
6.
7.
8.
9.
10.
11.
12.
13.
14.
15.
16.
17.

5. PARENT: Say each of the following phrases, one by one.
   Tell your CHILD to repeat each phrase after you:

"I now have 100 percent desire
that I am open and clear
and that only
pure and accurate and balanced energy
flow through my Being.
and we thank you."

## IF THIS IS THE FIRST TIME
you are playing the YOUMEES with your child,
continue on with the instructions in the ILLUMINATION.

◆ ◆ ◆

## IF THIS IS THE SECOND TIME
you are playing the YOUMEES with your child,
please refer to the Check-List of the YOUMEES you played
three months ago, in the first session,
to remember which YOUMEES you have already played.

## IN THIS SESSION,
you and your child will play
ALL the remaining YOUMEES
—the ones you did not play last time.

Since you already know
which YOUMEES you are going to play today,
skip over the rest of this ILLUMINATION,
and go directly to the INTENTION.

6. PARENT: Use another piece of paper to cut/tear 17 small slips of paper.

7. PARENT: Number each slip of paper, 1 through 17.

8. PARENT: Fold the slips of paper in half, so that the numbers are not showing, and lay them out on a table or on the floor, making sure that each of the 17 slips of paper is separated from all the other slips of paper.

9. PARENT: Pick up one of the slips of paper and hold it up in front of your CHILD, but do not open it, or look at the number written on it, or let your CHILD see the number on it.

10. PARENT: Tell your CHILD to look at the folded slip of paper you are holding, and tell your CHILD—for any reason, or for no reason at all—to hold up either one finger or two fingers.

> Tell your DAUGHTER to use the fingers of her RIGHT hand.

> Tell your SON to use the fingers of his LEFT hand.

>> What is happening here is that your child's intuitive "knowing" is at work. Without seeing the numbers on the pieces of paper, your CHILD's "Higher Self" is indicating which wounds (signified by number) should be healed at this particular session.

In the "Higher Self Code" that is being used here,
one finger means "Yes"
and two fingers means "No."

If, for any reason, your child is incapable of
or uncomfortable with holding up fingers,
you can act on behalf of your child.

If this is the case, you say,
"It is my intention to act now for my child in his/her highest interest.
Thee. Me. Me. Thee."

Then, select the folded slips of papers, one by one,
and without opening them or looking at the numbers on them,
hold up one or two fingers in response to each piece of paper.

For your DAUGHTER: Use the fingers of your RIGHT hand.
For your SON: Use the fingers of your LEFT hand.

11. PARENT: Put "one finger"—"Yes"—slips of paper in
one pile, and "two finger"—"No"—slips of paper in
another pile.

12. Continue this process through all 17 slips of paper:

Hold up piece of paper.

Your CHILD looks at piece of paper and
responds with one or two fingers.

YOU put each slip of paper in the one-finger
pile or in the two-finger pile.

13. PARENT: When the process has been completed with all 17 slips of paper, open the papers in the "one-finger"—"Yes"—pile.

> Put a check mark on your Check-List of 17 numbers next to every number from the papers in this "one-finger"—"Yes"—pile.

> The wounds that correspond to the numbers on the Check-List are the wounds that need healing at this particular session, and indicate which YOUMEES you and your child will play at this session.

Go on to the INTENTION.

# 4

# INTENTION

Just before beginning to play the first YOUMEE, PARENT and CHILD each take three deep breaths, inhaling and exhaling loudly, and then recite this INTENTION.

PARENT: Say the Intention-Words indicated for you to say, and then guide your CHILD to say the CHILD's Intention-Words by repeating after you.

> It may be easier for your CHILD if you recite the CHILD's Intention-Words a few words at a time, or, even, one-by-one.

> Continue this way until the entire INTENTION is complete.

PARENT: "We ask that the healing we are about to do be done with grace for the highest good of all involved."

CHILD: "We ask that the healing we are about to do be done with grace for the highest good of all involved."

PARENT: "We ask that transformation be allowed in all bodies simultaneously."

> Here the word "bodies" means the physical, mental, emotional, and spiritual bodies. You are asking that the healing take place in all those places (on all those levels) at the same time.

PARENT: "With wisdom and peace."

CHILD: "With wisdom and peace."

PARENT: "We thank you and we thank you."

CHILD: "We thank you and we thank you."

PARENT and CHILD each touch his/her wrists together (as though hands are in a praying position) and spread hands apart slightly (as though hands are in a catching position)

And together, PARENT and CHILD say:

## *Behold, Begin, Open*

Go on to the instructions for playing the YOUMEES.

# 5

# PLAYING THE YOUMEES

Play each YOUMEE that you have identified in the ILLUMINATION and marked on your Check-List, beginning with the lowest number on the Check-List, and continuing through the highest number on the Check-List.

Please remember:

Play each YOUMEE step-by-step, following the numbered instructions.

Follow each script-direction that is given to you, the PARENT.

Give your CHILD each script-direction that is indicated for your CHILD to say/do.

Carefully guide your CHILD through each instruction.

When you have completed all the YOUMEES
on your Check-List,
please be sure to turn to page 139 for
THE SEAL OF GRATITUDE
and then, if appropriate for your child, recite
THE LIMITATION RELEASE.
Then, recite THE ANCHOR
in order to close the session
and lock in the healing.
Finally, conclude by closing the Sacred Space.

Go on to play the first YOUMEE on your Check-List.

# ANGER

ANGER is a need to defend oneself, through attack,
against the harshness of this-world experience.

## BEHAVIOR

A child who is ANGRY may: throw tantrums, pound fists, pick
fights, refuse to join in or participate in activities, refuse to play by
the rules, be oppositional.

## IN THE PHYSICAL BODY

In the physical body, ANGER is centered in the RIGHT PALM.

Negative physical energy can come through the palm. When we
are angry, our hands, our palms, even involuntarily, make a fist
that is ready to lash out at the object of our anger.

This is affirmed by the old wives' tale that says that "if your palm
itches, you are going to be in a fight."

# ♦ YOUMEE I ♦

1. PARENT and CHILD sit on chairs facing one another.

2. PARENT and CHILD grasp hands (as if shaking hands).

   With a GIRL: PARENT and CHILD grasp RIGHT hands.

   With a BOY: PARENT and CHILD grasp LEFT hands.

3. CHILD gently pulls PARENT up from chair and pulls PARENT toward him/her.

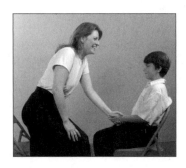

4.  PARENT (still holding the CHILD's hand) offers a little resist-
    ance, and then cooperates, gets up, and moves around CHILD
    to the back of the chair, moving in the direction of the
    CHILD's hand that is pulling.

    > With a GIRL: PARENT moves toward RIGHT
    > of CHILD.

    > With a BOY: PARENT moves toward LEFT of
    > CHILD.

5.  PARENT stands behind CHILD (who is still sitting on chair),
    still holding hands.

6.  Standing behind CHILD, PARENT whispers into CHILD's
    ear, "Your anger is healed."

    > Into GIRL's RIGHT ear.

    > Into BOY's LEFT ear.

7. PARENT returns to chair. The process is repeated, but in reverse.

> With a GIRL: Hold LEFT hand, move to LEFT, whisper in LEFT ear: "Your anger is healed."

> With a BOY: Hold RIGHT hand, move to RIGHT, whisper in RIGHT ear: "Your anger is healed."

8. PARENT and CHILD each touch his/her wrists together (as though hands are in a praying position) and spread hands apart slightly (as though hands are in a catching position)

And together, PARENT and CHILD say:

# Concluded, Complete, Discharged

Go on to play the next YOUMEE on your Check-List.
If this is the last YOUMEE on your Check-List,
please turn to page 139 to recite THE SEAL OF GRATITUDE.

# GRIEF

GRIEF is weeping at the separation.

## BEHAVIOR

A CHILD in GRIEF may: be sad, lethargic, may not eat, may not sleep, may not want to play, may do poorly in school, may lack motivation, may be withdrawn, fearful, angry, may deny or even punish him/herself.

## IN THE PHYSICAL BODY

In the physical body, GRIEF is centered in the THROAT.

In grief, we feel a "lump in our throats," our voices quiver, and our throats are "filled with tears."

# ◆ YOUMEE **2** ◆

1. PARENT and CHILD stand facing each other.

2. CHILD places his/her hands on top of PARENT's hands, palm to palm.

3. Keeping palms together, PARENT and CHILD walk clockwise in two full circles.

4. PARENT and CHILD stand still (each "at attention"; each with ankles touching), keeping their hands touching each other palm to palm.

5. PARENT says: "I invite you to release your grief."

6. CHILD says: "I am happy to release my grief."

7. PARENT and CHILD release hand-hold.

8.  PARENT puts hand in front of CHILD's throat (about six inches away) with fingers facing up.

    With a GIRL: PARENT uses RIGHT hand.

    With a BOY: PARENT uses LEFT hand.

9.  PARENT imagines energy flowing from hand to throat.

10. PARENT slowly moves hand three times in a clockwise circle at CHILD's throat with the intention (thinking about) of giving CHILD's throat an "energy boost."

11. PARENT holds hand steadily at CHILD's throat for another moment.

12. PARENT lowers hand.

13. With their hands at their sides, PARENT and CHILD do an 8 step circle dance—stepping exactly 8 times to make a full circle, so that the PARENT and CHILD each end up at his/her own starting position.

    With a GIRL: both PARENT and daughter start with RIGHT foot, and circle to right.

    With a BOY: both PARENT and son start with LEFT foot, and circle to left.

14. PARENT and CHILD each touch his/her wrists together (as though hands are in a praying position) and spread hands apart slightly (as though hands are in a catching position)

And together, PARENT and CHILD say:

## Concluded, Complete, Discharged

Go on to play the next YOUMEE on your Check-List.
If this is the last YOUMEE on your Check-List,
please turn to page 139 to recite THE SEAL OF GRATITUDE.

# FEAR

FEAR is the experience of being in danger
because of being too small, "too little."

## BEHAVIOR

A child who is in FEAR may: hide, panic, withdraw, cry, procras-
tinate, put off going places or doing things, engage in ritual behavior (such as not stepping on sidewalk cracks; habitual hand-wash-
ing), may have fears or phobias about certain things (such as
heights, narrow places, animals), may be clingy, may be afraid of
the dark, may have nightmares, may make up stories or tell lies.

## IN THE PHYSICAL BODY

In the physical body, FEAR is centered in the KIDNEYS.

In fear, our kidneys feel both acute pain and a long-lasting, dull
ache (especially in back) so that we are bent over, "doubled up," in
fear and pain.

In frightful, fearful moments, we involuntarily "let go" and we—
in the vernacular—"wet our pants."

# ♦ YOUMEE 3 ♦

1. PARENT and CHILD sit on chairs, back to back.

2. PARENT and CHILD, still back to back, both stand up, at the same time.

3. PARENT and CHILD imagine hugging each other and together say: "I am with you."

4. PARENT and CHILD, at the same time, jump up and down in place 3 times.

5. PARENT and CHILD, at the same time, sit down.

6. Together, PARENT and CHILD say: "You are mine."

7. PARENT and CHILD each touch his/her wrists together (as though hands are in a praying position) and spread hands apart slightly (as though hands are in a catching position)

And together, PARENT and CHILD say:

## *Concluded, Complete, Discharged*

Go on to play the next YOUMEE on your Check-List.
If this is the last YOUMEE on your Check-List,
please turn to page 139 to recite THE SEAL OF GRATITUDE.

# DISTRUST

DISTRUST is not being able to count on any reality as certain.

## BEHAVIOR

A child who DISTRUSTS may: lie, make up stories, may be afraid, not be forthcoming, may hold back information/expression of feelings, may lack motivation, test (self and others) on boundaries and limits, may display lack of confidence, lack of self-esteem, may withdraw, shy away from intimacy, may be unable to form close relationships.

## IN THE PHYSICAL BODY

In the physical body, DISTRUST is centered in the BACK OF THE KNEES.

When we distrust, the back of our knees hurt because we are always "on edge," sitting on the edge of our seats, ready to run, ready to flee.

# ◆ YOUMEE 4 ◆

1. PARENT and CHILD stand facing each other.

2. PARENT places hands on CHILD's shoulders.

3. Still with hands on shoulders, PARENT takes four steps.

   With a GIRL: Four steps to girl's RIGHT
   [PARENT's left].

   With a BOY: Four steps to boy's LEFT
   [PARENT's right].

4. Still with hands on shoulders, looking into the CHILD's eyes, the PARENT says: "You are love and joy."

5. CHILD says: "I am love and joy."

6. PARENT takes four steps back to original position.

7. PARENT puts hands down.

8. PARENT says: "You are precious and pure."

9.   CHILD says: "I am precious and pure."

10.  PARENT and CHILD each put hand in middle of his/her own chest, above the heart.

> With a GIRL: RIGHT hand.
>
> With a BOY: LEFT hand.
>
> The other hand remains by the side.

11.  PARENT and CHILD, at the same time, both bend knees slightly and bow from waist toward each other (being careful not to bump heads).

12. PARENT and CHILD each touch his/her wrists together (as though hands are in a praying position) and spread hands apart slightly (as though hands are in a catching position)

And together, PARENT and CHILD say:

# Concluded, Complete, Discharged

Go on to play the next YOUMEE on your Check-List.
If this is the last YOUMEE on your Check-List,
please turn to page 139 to recite THE SEAL OF GRATITUDE.

# DESPAIR

DESPAIR is giving up the connection to the breath of God.

## BEHAVIOR

A child who is in DESPAIR may: give up, withdraw, not try, may not eat, or sleep, may not follow directions or rules, may display anger.

## IN THE PHYSICAL BODY

In the physical body, DESPAIR is centered in the HEART.

When we are in despair, our heart aches, our heart is broken, our heart is attacked.

# ♦ YOUMEE 5 ♦

1. PARENT and CHILD sit side by side on a couch or on two chairs without arms so that their sides/hips/and shoulders are touching.

   PARENT sits on RIGHT side of a GIRL.

   PARENT sits on LEFT side of a BOY.

2. PARENT and CHILD each put both hands on his/her heart.

   GIRL and PARENT of GIRL: RIGHT hand on chest; LEFT hand on top of right.

   BOY and PARENT of BOY: LEFT hand on chest; RIGHT hand on top of left.

3.  In unison, PARENT and CHILD take two deep breaths, inhaling and exhaling loudly (making sounds like big sighs).

4.  PARENT says: "I feel the tears of your heart."

5.  PARENT removes his/her hands from heart and puts one hand on CHILD's back, directly behind heart.

    With a GIRL: PARENT puts LEFT hand.

    With a BOY: PARENT puts RIGHT hand.

    CHILD's hands remain on his/her heart.

6.  PARENT says: "I send your tears into the light of my love."

7.  PARENT and CHILD each touch his/her wrists together (as though hands are in a praying position) and spread hands apart slightly (as though hands are in a catching position)

    And together, PARENT and CHILD say:

# Concluded, Complete, Discharged

Go on to play the next YOUMEE on your Check-List.
If this is the last YOUMEE on your Check-List,
please turn to page 139 to recite THE SEAL OF GRATITUDE.

# ANGUISH

**ANGUISH is the belief in aloneness.**

## BEHAVIOR

A child who is ANGUISHED may: be anxious, distressed, tearful, may "wring" his/her hands, may have little tolerance, may not be able to focus or concentrate, may be easily frustrated, may worry, may have a hard time sleeping.

## IN THE PHYSICAL BODY

In the physical body, ANGUISH is centered in the LOWER INTESTINES.

When we are in anguish, we are "tied up in knots," our "guts are wrenched." Our "bowels are in an uproar."

# ♦ YOUMEE 6 ♦

1. PARENT and CHILD stand facing each other.

2. PARENT and CHILD each take two steps away from the other.

   A GIRL and PARENT each take two steps to her/his own LEFT.

   A BOY and PARENT each take two steps to his/her own RIGHT.

3. PARENT and CHILD are now standing diagonally across from each other.

   However, they do not face each other diagonally, but, rather, each stands facing straight ahead.

4. PARENT says: "Let go of your anguish."

5. CHILD says: "I let go."

6.   PARENT and CHILD each make a one-quarter turn so that they are now facing each other on the diagonal.

7.   PARENT and CHILD walk toward each other and meet.

8.   PARENT and CHILD hug.

     PARENT hugs CHILD around the shoulders.

     CHILD hugs PARENT around the waist.

9.   While they hug, PARENT says: "You are free."

10. When the hug is over, PARENT and CHILD each touch his/her wrists together (as though hands are in a praying position) and spread hands apart slightly (as though hands are in a catching position)

And together, PARENT and CHILD say:

## Concluded, Complete, Discharged

Go on to play the next YOUMEE on your Check-List.
If this is the last YOUMEE on your Check-List,
please turn to page 139 to recite THE SEAL OF GRATITUDE.

# SHAME

SHAME is being embarrassed in front of the whole cosmos.

## BEHAVIOR

A child who is ASHAMED may: withdraw, not want to "show self," not want to participate, may be self-punishing, may experience embarrassment, fear exposure, hide away.

## IN THE PHYSICAL BODY

In the physical body, SHAME is centered in the LEFT INNER EAR.

When we are ashamed, we do not want to hear, we do not want to receive. Our ears are "closed." Our ears "burn" with shame. Our internal equilibrium—centered in the inner ear—is off balance.

# ♦ YOUMEE 7 ♦

1.  PARENT and CHILD stand side by side.

    PARENT stands on the right side of a GIRL.

    PARENT stands on the left side of a BOY.

2.  PARENT and CHILD take four steps to the side.

    With a GIRL: Four steps to the RIGHT.

    With a BOY: Four steps to the LEFT.

3.  PARENT, in a sing-song, says: "We have pride in you. We have pride in you."

4.  PARENT and CHILD put arms "around each other."

> With a GIRL: PARENT's left arm goes around GIRL's shoulder; GIRL's right arm goes around PARENT's waist.

> With a BOY: PARENT's right arm goes around BOY's shoulder; BOY's left arm goes around PARENT's waist.

5.  PARENT, in a sing-song, says: "Hear that we are proud of you. Hear that we are proud of you."

6.  PARENT and CHILD lower arms to sides.

7.  CHILD, in a sing-song, says: "I hear that you are proud of me. I hear that you are proud of me."

8.  PARENT and CHILD put arms around each other again (in same way as before).

9.  CHILD, in a sing-song, says: "I have pride in me. I have pride in me."

10. PARENT and CHILD lower arms to sides.

11. PARENT and CHILD each touch his/her wrists together (as though hands are in a praying position) and spread hands apart slightly (as though hands are in a catching position)

And together, PARENT and CHILD say:

## Concluded, Complete, Discharged

Go on to play the next YOUMEE on your Check-List.
If this is the last YOUMEE on your Check-List,
please turn to page 139 to recite THE SEAL OF GRATITUDE.

# INSECURITY

INSECURITY is the experience of having no solid ground inside.

## BEHAVIOR

A child who is INSECURE may: have an upset stomach or complain of a "tummy ache," may be clingy, exhibit compulsive traits, have fears, have trouble going to sleep at night, may withdraw and hold back or exhibit false bravado, may lie, brag, exaggerate, may spend a lot of time in a fantasy world.

## IN THE PHYSICAL BODY

In the physical body, INSECURITY is centered in the STOMACH.

When we are insecure, our stomach is upset. We "have butterflies." Our stomach "does flip flops." We often have to "run to the bathroom."

# ◆ YOUMEE 8 ◆

1.  PARENT and CHILD stand back to back.

2.  PARENT reaches hand back and grasps CHILD's hand.

    With a GIRL: PARENT reaches with left hand; grasps GIRL's RIGHT hand.

    With a BOY: PARENT reaches with right hand; grasps BOY's LEFT hand.

3.  Holding hands, PARENT and CHILD pivot and face each other.

4.  PARENT and CHILD lift their held hands up overhead. Other hand is at side.

5.  CHILD gently pulls (moves) PARENT around the front of his/her body and twirls PARENT all the way around his/her body (as if PARENT is circling a Maypole).

6.  PARENT and CHILD drop hands to sides and release the hand-hold.

7.  PARENT, in a sing-song, says to CHILD: "Whole and strong are you."

8.  PARENT and CHILD grasp hands again, this time with the opposite hand.

    With a GIRL: PARENT uses RIGHT hand; GIRL uses LEFT hand.

With a BOY: PARENT uses LEFT hand; BOY uses RIGHT hand.

9.   PARENT and CHILD lift their held hands up overhead.

10. CHILD gently pulls (moves) PARENT around the front of his/her body and twirls PARENT all the way around his her/body (as if PARENT is circling a Maypole).

   Because PARENT and CHILD are holding opposite hands from the first time, the twirl will be in the opposite direction.

11. PARENT and CHILD drop hands to sides and release the hand-hold.

12. PARENT puts hands on CHILD's shoulders, and, again, in a sing-song, says to CHILD: "Whole and strong are you."

13. PARENT and CHILD each touch his/her wrists together (as though hands are in a praying position) and spread hands apart slightly (as though hands are in a catching position)

And together, PARENT and CHILD say:

# Concluded, Complete, Discharged

Go on to play the next YOUMEE on your Check-List.
If this is the last YOUMEE on your Check-List,
please turn to page 139 to recite THE SEAL OF GRATITUDE.

# SELFISHNESS

SELFISHNESS is the fear of coming out to interact
with this-world experience.

## BEHAVIOR

A child who is SELFISH may: not share things or thoughts or feelings, may hoard, be stingy, keep things to him/herself, may be
closed off, may look/seem withdrawn, may explode in anger
(closed off, closed off, closed off, BAM!).

The opposite of selfishness is not generosity, but inter-acting.

## IN THE PHYSICAL BODY

In the physical body, SELFISHNESS is centered in the BACK OF
THE HEELS.

When we are selfish, we "dig in our heels" and hoard or protect
what is ours. We are often "off balance," "rock on our heels," and
"fall flat on our faces."

# ♦ YOUMEE 9 ♦

1.  PARENT sits on chair; CHILD stands in back of chair, facing PARENT's back.

2.  CHILD moves to the side of PARENT.

    A GIRL: moves to the PARENT's RIGHT.

    A BOY: moves to the PARENT's LEFT.

3. CHILD pivots to face PARENT, who is still sitting on the chair, but is still facing straight ahead.

That means that the CHILD is facing the PARENT's side.

4. PARENT says: "I cannot see you."

5. CHILD says: "I am here."

6. PARENT says: "Where?"

7. CHILD says: "Here."

8. PARENT, still sitting in chair, pivots to face CHILD.

9. CHILD moves/scampers to stand behind PARENT:

The direction in which the CHILD moves/scampers does not matter.

CHILD is now standing behind the PARENT who is still sitting on the chair.

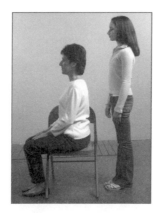

10. CHILD again moves to the side of the PARENT (to the opposite side where he/she stood before).

> A GIRL moves to and stands on PARENT's LEFT.

> A BOY moves to and stands on PARENT's RIGHT.

11. CHILD pivots to face PARENT.

12. PARENT and CHILD repeat the dialogue.

> PARENT says: "I cannot see you."
> CHILD says: "I am here."
> PARENT says: "Where?"
> CHILD says: "Here."

13. PARENT turns in chair to face CHILD.

14. PARENT looks at CHILD and says: "I see you."

15. CHILD looks at PARENT and says: "I am here."

16. PARENT, still looking at CHILD, says: "Thank you."

17. CHILD, still looking at PARENT, says: "You're welcome."

18. PARENT and CHILD each touch his/her wrists together (as though hands are in a praying position) and spread hands apart slightly (as though hands are in a catching position)

And together, PARENT and CHILD say:

## Concluded, Complete, Discharged

Go on to play the next YOUMEE on your Check-List.
If this is the last YOUMEE on your Check-List,
please turn to page 139 to recite THE SEAL OF GRATITUDE.

# LOSS

LOSS is not being able to find one's own heart.

## BEHAVIOR

A child who is experiencing LOSS may: be clingy, clutchy, may hold on, hoard, may become a "pack-rat," may be overly responsible, may become a "little parent."

## IN THE PHYSICAL BODY

In the physical body, LOSS is centered in the LUNGS.

When we experience loss, we experience shortness of breath, we cannot "catch our breath," we gasp for air. Our lungs are congested; our lungs are "filled with tears." We often display symptoms of asthma or other respiratory ailments.

# ◆ YOUMEE 10 ◆

1.  PARENT and CHILD sit facing each other.

2.  PARENT holds right hand in front of CHILD's chest/lungs.

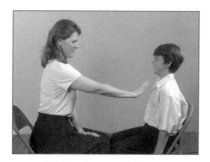

3.  PARENT makes clockwise circles in front of CHILD's chest/lungs.

4.  The circles get smaller and smaller until the PARENT imagines pulling all the loss out of the CHILD's lungs.

5.  PARENT throws all the loss behind him/her (continuing to pull and throw, pull and throw).

6. While pulling and throwing, the PARENT says: "I release all loss from you."

7. CHILD says: "I release all loss from me."

8. PARENT repeats the pulling and throwing until the PARENT feels that all the loss is gone from the CHILD's lungs.

9. PARENT and CHILD each put his/her hands on his/her lap.

10. PARENT says: "You are filled with light and love."

11. CHILD says: "I am filled with light and love."

12. CHILD places hands over lungs (one hand on top of the other).

    A GIRL: puts RIGHT hand directly on lungs, left hand on top of right hand.

    A BOY: puts LEFT hand directly on lungs, right hand on top of left hand.

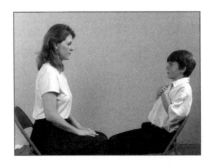

13. PARENT places his/her hands on top of CHILD's hands.

   With a GIRL: PARENT places RIGHT hand on top of GIRL's hands and then places left hand on top of right hand.

   With a BOY: PARENT places LEFT hand on top of BOY's hands and then places right hand on top of left hand.

14. CHILD and PARENT hold hands in place for a few moments, while the PARENT imagines/feels putting light and love into the CHILD's lungs.

   Hands are held in place for as long as it feels good and right to the PARENT.

15. PARENT and CHILD put hands back on lap.

16. PARENT and CHILD each touch his/her wrists together (as though hands are in a praying position) and spread hands apart slightly (as though hands are in a catching position)

And together, PARENT and CHILD say:

# Concluded, Complete, Discharged

Go on to play the next YOUMEE on your Check-List.
If this is the last YOUMEE on your Check-List,
please turn to page 139 to recite THE SEAL OF GRATITUDE.

# PANIC

PANIC is the experience of being suspended in mid-air
with nothing to grasp or hold on to.

## BEHAVIOR

A child who is experiencing PANIC may: be anxious, have trouble
sleeping, have nightmares, may cry easily, have little tolerance, a
low level of frustration, may have eating disorders, may be enuret-
ic (that is, wets his/her pants), may get sick easily (or have low levels of resistance to physical illness).

## IN THE PHYSICAL BODY

In the physical body, PANIC is centered in the ADRENALS.

The adrenals are physically linked to the kidneys, which makes
sense because panic and fear are twins.

When we panic, our adrenals go into "high gear," giving us a surge
of physical energy and strength to combat the panic. The adrenals
release adrenaline to give us the power to "fight or flee."

# ◆ YOUMEE II ◆

1.  PARENT sits on a chair; CHILD stands behind PARENT, facing PARENT's back.

2.  CHILD says: "I cannot find you."

3.  PARENT says: "I am here."

4.  CHILD says: "Where?"

5.  PARENT says: "Here."

6. PARENT turns to the side.

    With a GIRL: PARENT turns to the RIGHT.

    With a BOY: PARENT turns to the LEFT.

7. CHILD says: "Where are you?"

8. PARENT says: "Here."

9. PARENT (continuing) says: "Where are YOU?"

10. CHILD says: "Here."

11. PARENT stands up, moves chair to face CHILD, and again sits on chair, now facing CHILD.

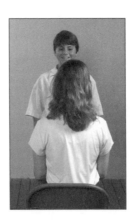

12. PARENT puts arms/hands around CHILD, so that hands are on CHILD's lower back (in the area of the adrenals).

13. PARENT looks into CHILD's eyes and says: "You are found."

14. CHILD says: "I am found."

15. PARENT releases arms/hands from around CHILD.

16. PARENT and CHILD each touch his/her wrists together (as though hands are in a praying position) and spread hands apart slightly (as though hands are in a catching position)

And together, PARENT and CHILD say:

## Concluded, Complete, Discharged

Go on to play the next YOUMEE on your Check-List.
If this is the last YOUMEE on your Check-List,
please turn to page 139 to recite THE SEAL OF GRATITUDE.

# INFERIORITY

INFERIORITY is the belief "I'll never be as good as God."

## BEHAVIOR

A child who feels INFERIOR may: be constricted in movements and activities, may hang back, "disappear" (this means that the child feels "not seen" by others), may be afraid but does not say anything about being afraid and does not admit to fear, may be shy, easily embarrassed, self-deprecating, self-critical, may write in a cramped style.

## IN THE PHYSICAL BODY

In the physical body, INFERIORITY is centered in the CHEST.

When we feel inferior, we feel constricted. There is a tightness in our chest, and we feel as if we cannot move, as if moving too quickly or too far widens our circle and exposes us too much. We feel as if there is a "vise around our chests," and that we are being pounded and squeezed.

# ◆ YOUMEE 12 ◆

1.  PARENT and CHILD kneel side by side.

    With a GIRL: PARENT is on GIRL's RIGHT side.

    With a BOY: PARENT is on BOY's LEFT side.

2.  PARENT and CHILD raise hands straight up over their heads.

3.  PARENT and CHILD bring hands back toward to their sides.

4.  PARENT and CHILD stand up, each holding his/her hands at side.

5.  PARENT says: "You are the best."

6. PARENT and CHILD hold hands.

   With a GIRL: PARENT uses left hand to hold GIRL's RIGHT hand.

   With a BOY: PARENT uses right hand to hold BOY's LEFT hand.

7. PARENT and CHILD "step dance" in a circle.

   With a GIRL: Both PARENT and CHILD start by putting LEFT foot over right and continue in the circling step dance by continuing to put left foot over right.

   With a BOY: Both PARENT and CHILD start by putting RIGHT foot over left and continue in the circling step dance by continuing to put right foot over left.

8. As they step dance in the circle, PARENT and CHILD swing their arms back and forth and in a sing-song, say together: "You are the best."

   The sentence is repeated over and over until the dance is completed, full circle.

9. When they have come full circle, PARENT and CHILD stop. They continue to hold hands.

10. CHILD says: "I am the best."

11. PARENT and CHILD repeat the dance, swinging their arms, starting with the opposite foot than the last dance, thus circling in the opposite direction.

> With a GIRL: PARENT and CHILD start by putting RIGHT foot over left and continue in the circling dance step by continuing to put right foot over left.

> With a BOY: PARENT and CHILD start by putting LEFT foot over right and continue in the circling dance step by continuing to put left foot over right.

12. While doing the circle step dance, PARENT and CHILD say, in a sing-song: "I am the best."

    The sentence is repeated over and over until dance is completed, full circle.

13. When they have come full circle, PARENT and CHILD stop.

14. PARENT and CHILD each touch his/her wrists together (as though hands are in a praying position) and spread hands apart slightly (as though hands are in a catching position)

And together, PARENT and CHILD say:

## Concluded, Complete, Discharged

Go on to play the next YOUMEE on your Check-List.
If this is the last YOUMEE on your Check-List,
please turn to page 139 to recite THE SEAL OF GRATITUDE.

# HATRED

Hatred is the experience of feeling as though
one does not deserve re-union.

## BEHAVIOR

A child who HATES may: be a perfectionist, be critical, may separate self from others, may see things in extremes (blacks and whites) with little middle ground, may be angry, hit, fight, push away, may be foul-mouthed, spew incendiary words, may be prejudiced, bigoted, put down others.

## IN THE PHYSICAL BODY

In the physical body, HATRED is centered in the LIVER.

The liver is the seat of our most primordial and primal feelings and reactions. The liver can hold our fears, our anger, our most hateful feelings.

When our liver holds too much hatred, our entire system is affected; poisons can invade our whole body. We are filled with bile—the foul-acting, foul-tasting internal juices of pain and loathing.

Since we cannot function without a liver, when the liver breaks down, we can die. So, releasing and healing the hatred that lives in our liver is, literally, a matter of life or death.

# ◆ YOUMEE 13 ◆

1.  CHILD stands in front of a chair, facing forward.

2.  PARENT stands behind chair, facing CHILD's back.

3.  PARENT says: "You are adored."

4.  CHILD sits on chair.

5.  PARENT continues to stand behind the chair, behind the CHILD, facing the CHILD's back.

6.  PARENT says: "You are one with the universe."

7.  CHILD says: "The universe is one with me."

8.   PARENT gently taps CHILD on the top of the head several times.

>   With a GIRL: PARENT taps with RIGHT hand.

>   With a BOY: PARENT taps with LEFT hand.

9.   CHILD stands up and then stands on the chair, facing PARENT.

10.  PARENT says: "We are one."

11.  CHILD says: "We are one."

12. PARENT and CHILD both stretch out their arms to their sides.

13. PARENT says: "We are love."

14. CHILD says: "We are love."

15. PARENT and CHILD lower hands to their sides.

16. CHILD gets off chair.

17. CHILD stands in front of chair facing PARENT. The chair is still between them.

18. Together, PARENT and CHILD move the chair from between them and set it to one side. It does not matter which side.

19. Together, PARENT and CHILD say: "We are wonderful."

20. PARENT and CHILD each touch his/her wrists together (as though hands are in a praying position) and spread hands apart slightly (as though hands are in a catching position)


And together, PARENT and CHILD say:

## *Concluded, Complete, Discharged*


Go on to play the next YOUMEE on your Check-List.
If this is the last YOUMEE on your Check-List,
please turn to page 139 to recite THE SEAL OF GRATITUDE.

# INDIGNATION

INDIGNATION is holding righteousness in response
to the lack of dignity expressed for God's creatures.

## BEHAVIOR

A child who is INDIGNANT may: be self-righteous, angry, may
have a need to get even, may want revenge for slights real and
imagined, may act as if strict justice outweighs mercy/compas-
sion, may act as if the concept of justice is more important than
the people involved.

## IN THE PHYSICAL BODY

In the physical body, INDIGNATION is centered in the RIGHT HIP.

When our hip is bruised or broken, our forward progress is
impeded. We cannot move smoothly and effortlessly; instead we
limp and falter. Our steps are hobbled. Everything and anything
seems to block our way.

We are so concerned with the "small pebbles" on the path and how
they can hinder us that we lose sight of our goal, thinking that
there is nothing ahead that is worth pursuing. Eventually, we are
"drained"; we become unsteady and worn out.

# ◆ YOUMEE 14 ◆

1. PARENT and CHILD sit on the floor, across the room from each other, diagonally across from each other, facing each other, with legs stretched out in front of themselves.

2. Together, PARENT and CHILD say: "I am goodness."

3. PARENT and CHILD engage in a "shouting contest," trying to outshout each other.

4. CHILD says: "**I** am goodness."

5. PARENT says: "**I** am goodness."

6. CHILD says: "**I** am goodness."

7. CHILD stands up.

8. CHILD claps 3 times.

9. PARENT stands up.

10. PARENT claps 3 times.

11. PARENT and CHILD alternate taking steps forward, one by one, until they meet in the middle of the room.

    CHILD leads the walking.

If the CHILD takes a regular step, then the PARENT takes a regular step.

If the CHILD takes a "baby step," then the PARENT takes a "baby step."

If the CHILD takes a "giant step," then the PARENT takes a "giant step."

12. CHILD steps forward one step.

   A GIRL: Steps with RIGHT foot first.

   A BOY: Steps with LEFT foot first.

13. PARENT steps forward one step.

   With a GIRL: PARENT steps with RIGHT foot first.

   With a BOY: PARENT steps with LEFT foot first.

14. PARENT and CHILD continue taking alternate steps until they meet.

15. PARENT and CHILD grasp hands.

16. PARENT and CHILD hold hands and walk in a half-circle until each is standing in the other's place.

> With a GIRL: Parent and child begin the walk with the RIGHT foot.

> With a BOY: Parent and child begin the walk with the LEFT foot.

>> CHILD now stands where the PARENT began the half-circle walk.

>> PARENT now stands where the CHILD began the half-circle walk.

17. When PARENT and CHILD have reached the new position on the half-circle, still holding hands, together PARENT and CHILD say: "We are right."

18. Still holding hands, PARENT and CHILD again walk forward in a half-circle until each is standing in his/her original place.

   > With a GIRL: PARENT and CHILD again begin the walk with the RIGHT foot.

   > With a BOY: PARENT and CHILD again begin the walk with the LEFT foot.

19. Together, PARENT and CHILD say: "We are right."

20. PARENT and CHILD release hands from hand-hold.

21. PARENT and CHILD each touch his/her wrists together (as though hands are in a praying position) and spread hands apart slightly (as though hands are in a catching position)

And together, PARENT and CHILD say:

## Concluded, Complete, Discharged

Go on to play the next YOUMEE on your Check-List.
If this is the last YOUMEE on your Check-List,
please turn to page 139 to recite THE SEAL OF GRATITUDE.

# RESENTMENT

RESENTMENT is the wish that the world
matches the inner vision.

## BEHAVIOR

A child who is RESENTFUL may: be angry, bitter, may carry a
grudge, may compare and find fault, may be critical of others, may
inflate sense of self, may demand special treatment.

## IN THE PHYSICAL BODY

In the physical body, RESENTMENT is centered in the GALL-
BLADDER.

When we are resentful, we are suffused with bitterness. We are
deeply offended; our pride is damaged and we are filled with gall.
When too much resentment overwhelms us, sometimes we lose
our temper and lash out.

Yet often, we harbor our malice, and increase our irritation. That
irritation can turn into gallstones, which reflect our rage and are
painful to pass.

# ◆ YOUMEE 15 ◆

1.  PARENT and CHILD sit on chairs, back to back.

2.  PARENT and CHILD each folds his/her arms over chest, as if in a stubborn or angry gesture.

3.  PARENT and CHILD unfold arms, and stand up, still back to back.

4.  PARENT and CHILD each take two steps forward.

5.  PARENT and CHILD each put hands on hips.

6.  PARENT and CHILD turn around and face each other.

7.  With hands still on hips, PARENT and CHILD walk in circles around the chairs.

    With a GIRL: PARENT and CHILD begin walking with RIGHT foot first and circle right.

    With a BOY: PARENT and CHILD begin walking with LEFT foot first and circle left.

8.  As they keep walking in circles around the chairs, PARENT and CHILD "eye each other."

    This is like playing a game of musical chairs except instead of the stopped music being the signal to sit, the CHILD makes the decision when and on which chair to sit.

9.  When CHILD decides he/she wants to sit, he/she picks a chair and sits.

10. PARENT quickly sits on other chair.

11. If the CHILD chooses, PARENT and CHILD repeat the process:

> Sit on chairs, back to back
>
> Fold arms over chest
>
> Unfold arms
>
> Stand up—still back to back
>
> Take two steps forward
>
> Place hands on hips
>
> Turn around and face each other
>
> With hands still on hips, begin walking in circles around the chair.
>
>> With a GIRL: PARENT and CHILD—RIGHT foot first and circle right.
>>
>> With a BOY: PARENT and CHILD—LEFT foot first and circle left.
>
> CHILD decides when and on which chair to sit.
>
> PARENT quickly sits on other chair.

12. This process is repeated for as many times as the CHILD wishes to continue playing the game.

13. When the CHILD no longer wishes to repeat the process, he/she takes hands off hips and puts them on lap.

14. PARENT takes hands off hips and puts them on lap.

15. CHILD reaches hand in back of him/herself, and grasps PARENT's hand.

> A GIRL: Reaches back with RIGHT hand; PARENT grasps with left hand.
>
> A BOY: Reaches back with LEFT hand; PARENT grasps with right hand.

16. PARENT says: "You are deserving."

17. PARENT and CHILD reach back and grasp each other's other hand. They are now holding both hands.

18. CHILD says: "I am deserving."

19. Together, PARENT and CHILD say: "Light fills my soul."

20. PARENT and CHILD release hand-holds.

21. PARENT and CHILD each touch his/her wrists together (as though hands are in a praying position) and spread hands apart slightly (as though hands are in a catching position)


And together, PARENT and CHILD say:

# Concluded, Complete, Discharged


Go on to play the next YOUMEE on your Check-List.
If this is the last YOUMEE on your Check-List,
please turn to page 139 to recite THE SEAL OF GRATITUDE.

# JEALOUSY

**JEALOUSY is wanting what the angels have.**

## BEHAVIOR

A child who is JEALOUS may: be angry, may fight, may tattle-tale, may be mean and nasty, may bribe, flatter, "kiss up," "brown-nose," "suck up," day-dream.

## IN THE PHYSICAL BODY

In the physical body, JEALOUSY is centered BELOW THE EYES.

When we are jealous, our eyes covet, they envision us in places and circumstances different from reality.

The places below our eyes ache with envy. Our sinuses are irritated and filled with annoying pressure.

# ◆ YOUMEE 16 ◆

1. PARENT and CHILD are side by side on their hands and knees in a crawling position.

    > It does not matter which side PARENT and CHILD are on.

2. CHILD says: "Would you hold me?"

3. PARENT says: "Of course."

4. PARENT and CHILD move so that PARENT can hold CHILD.

5. PARENT holds CHILD depending on age of CHILD and how CHILD wants to be held.

    > Without using words, the CHILD moves to show the PARENT how he/she would like to be held.

    > The choice of how he/she is held is entirely up to the CHILD.

    > One CHILD may want to sit on PARENT's lap and be held.

    > Another CHILD may want to stand face to face with PARENT and be hugged and held.

    > Still another CHILD may want to stand side by side, with PARENT's arms around his/her shoulders and waist.

6.  When the holding is complete (the CHILD determines how long the holding takes place and when it is over), PARENT and CHILD stand side by side.

    It does not matter on which side PARENT and CHILD stand.

7.  CHILD says: "Would you hold my tears?"

8.  PARENT says: "Of course."

9.  PARENT and CHILD turn and face each other.

10. PARENT looks into CHILD's eyes with the intention of (thinking about) "taking the CHILD's tears" into his/her own eyes.

    PARENT continues the looking and intention for as long as the PARENT desires/needs.

11. When the looking and intention is complete, PARENT and CHILD turn and, once again stand side by side.

12. PARENT and CHILD now exchange places. They are still standing side by side, but in the opposite place from where they were just standing.

    This means that the PARENT is now standing where the CHILD stood, and

    The CHILD is now standing where the PARENT stood.

13. CHILD says: "Would you hold my dreams?"

14. PARENT says: "Of course."

15. PARENT and CHILD turn and face one another.

16. CHILD cups hands together.

17. PARENT holds CHILD's hands by cupping his/her hands underneath CHILD's, as if holding the CHILD's dreams.

Hands are held in this cupped position for as long as it feels good and right to both PARENT and CHILD.

PARENT and CHILD end the holding by silent mutual decision.

18. PARENT and CHILD put hands down to sides.

19. PARENT says: "You are perfect. You have everything."

20. PARENT and CHILD each touch his/her wrists together (as though hands are in a praying position) and spread hands apart slightly (as though hands are in a catching position)

And together, PARENT and CHILD say:

# Concluded, Complete, Discharged

Go on to play the next YOUMEE on your Check-List.
If this is the last YOUMEE on your Check-List,
please turn to page 139 to recite THE SEAL OF GRATITUDE.

# GUILT

GUILT is holding oneself responsible
or the lack of perfection in the world.

## BEHAVIOR

A child who is GUILTY may: sneak around, hide, may not want to
be found out, may withdraw, distrust others, may not sleep, may
have nightmares, may isolate self from others and from activities,
may lie, make up stories, attempt to over-compensate (in order to
control), may self-punish.

## IN THE PHYSICAL BODY

In the physical body, GUILT is centered in the RIGHT SHOULDER
JOINT.

When we are guilty, we are carrying a heavy burden. The "weight
of the world" is on our shoulders. We are pushed down and
brought low.

# ◆ YOUMEE 17 ◆

1.  PARENT sits on a chair.

2.  CHILD stands in front of PARENT, facing PARENT.

3.  CHILD says: "It is my fault."

4.  PARENT says: "You are free."

5.  PARENT stands up.

6.  PARENT "sweeps" the CHILD (makes sweeping motion) with
    hands from top to bottom (head to toe) as if there were dark
    clouds around CHILD that have to be swept away.

    The "sweeping" takes place in this order:

    With a GIRL:
    1.  Front of CHILD
    2.  Right side
    3.  Left side
    4.  Back

With a BOY:

1. Front of CHILD

2. Left side

3.  Right side

4.  Back

With both a GIRL and a BOY:

1.   Top of head (as high up as PARENT's arms can reach)

While doing the "head sweep," PARENT walks around the CHILD in a circle.

7.  At the conclusion of the full "sweep" of the CHILD, PARENT is now standing in front of CHILD again.

8.  PARENT says: "Your burdens are lifted."

9.  PARENT and CHILD both raise arms upward, until arms are overhead in the shape of a "V."

> To do this, PARENT and CHILD both hold arms straight out from their sides, like wings, and lift arms from sides until arms are overhead, forming the "V" overhead.

10. CHILD says: "My burdens are lifted."

11. PARENT and CHILD lower arms to sides.

12. PARENT and CHILD each touch his/her wrists together (as though hands are in a praying position) and spread hands apart slightly (as though hands are in a catching position)

And together, PARENT and CHILD say:

## *Concluded, Complete, Discharged*

This is the last YOUMEE that can be on your Check-List.
Please turn to page 139 to recite THE SEAL OF GRATITUDE.

# 6

# THE SEAL OF GRATITUDE

When PARENT and CHILD have completed the last YOUMEE designated for this session, you both take three deep breaths, inhaling and exhaling loudly, and then recite this SEAL OF GRATITUDE.

PARENT: "I now invite in health and peace."

CHILD: "I now invite in health and peace."

PARENT: "And I thank you with wisdom and peace."

CHILD: "And I thank you with wisdom and peace."

PARENT AND CHILD TOGETHER:
　"We pray
　that the sacred process we are involved with
　be manifest with grace and love
　for the highest good of all involved."

PARENT and CHILD each touch his/her wrists together (as though hands are in a praying position) and spread hands apart slightly (as though hands are in a catching position)

And together, PARENT and CHILD say:

*Concluded Completely,*
*With Love and Peace,*
*With Ease and Grace,*
*Completely Concluded,*
*Discharged*

If you sense that your child is a PLATINUM INDIGO
who is CARRYING A MEMORY IMPACT, go on to THE LIMITATION RELEASE.
Otherwise, go on to THE ANCHOR.

# 7

# THE LIMITATION RELEASE

IF you sense that your child is a **PLATINUM INDIGO** who is **CARRYING A MEMORY IMPACT,** instruct your child to recite this **LIMITATION RELEASE.**

"I now completely release
all limitation
imposed upon my Being
by the memories I carry."

INSTRUCT YOUR CHILD: To touch his/her wrists together (as though hands are in a praying position) and spread hands apart slightly (as though hands are in a catching position)

And say:

## *Concluded, Complete, Discharged*

Go on to THE ANCHOR.

# 8

# THE ANCHOR

Following the recitation of the SEAL OF GRATITUDE, PARENT and CHILD recite this ANCHOR. This Declaration locks in the healings and makes them permanent.

PARENT and CHILD together:

"Let there Be
Complete Circuitry
in all Bodies and Expressions."

**Breathe deeply.**

"Let there Be
Complete Transformation
in all Bodies and Expressions."

**Breathe deeply.**

"Let there Be
Complete Harmony
in all Bodies and Expressions."

**Breathe deeply.**

"Now and Forever."

**Breathe deeply.**

"Let It Be."

**Breathe deeply.**

PARENT and CHILD each touch his/her wrists together (as though hands are in a praying position) and spread hands apart slightly (as though hands are in a catching position)

And together, PARENT and CHILD say:

## *In Sacred Light*

This concludes this YOUMEE session.
CONGRATULATIONS to you and your child!
This would be the perfect time to give your child
the little gift of a stone, or a seashell, or a piece of driftwood.

In order to help ensure your continuing spiritual health and well-being,
please remember to close the Sacred Space.

# 9

# CLOSING SACRED SPACE

After you have completed playing the YOUMEES,
please remember to close the Sacred Space
by removing the Earth Element symbols
from the room.

Although it feels very good to "sit in the Light,"
if you stay for too long, it is exhausting;
it takes up too much of your "soul Energy."

When you remove the symbols, you return the space
to the 3-dimensional plane,
and you reclaim YourSelf and your full capacity
to function on this Earth plane.

**If this is the first time you and your child have played the YOUMEES, go on to read AND NOW on the page 145.**

This will remind you of the steps to take to play the YOUMEES with your child three months from now in order to achieve full healing of all these 17 spiritual woundings.

If this is the second time
you and your child have played the YOUMEES,
we join your child in thanking you
for guiding this sacred process,
which brings the blessings of spiritual healing
and Divine Light and Love.

You and your child will sense
if and when it is time for
a "BOOSTER" YOUMEE session.

If and when that times comes,
begin the YOUMEE process again
from the very beginning.

# AND NOW

## PLEASE REMEMBER

1.  KEEP THE CHECK-LIST on which you marked the YOUMEES that you and your child played today. In this way, you will remember which YOUMEES you have played and which YOUMEES are left to be played in three months.

2.  MARK YOUR CALENDAR. Make an appointment with yourself THREE MONTHS FROM NOW for another YOUMEE session.

3.  PLAY THE YOUMEES AGAIN. Three months after playing the YOUMEES for the first time, play the YOUMEES again.

    > At this second session, play the YOUMEE games for ALL the remaining spiritual woundings—the woundings that were not Illuminated the first time the YOUMEES were played.

    > At the conclusion of the second session, ALL 17 YOUMEES will have been played, and ALL 17 of these spiritual woundings will have been healed.

    > You and your child will sense if and when it is time for a "BOOSTER" YOUMEE session.

    > If and when that times comes, begin the YOUMEE process again from the very beginning.

# FINE TUNING

## The Word of Guidance

Sometimes, despite all our expectations, it will seem as if the YOUMEE session has not resulted in any change of attitudes or behavior for your child.

Guidance teaches that something in the child's energy field may be inhibiting the spiritual healing.

Here are a few possibilities of what may be blocking the way to healing, and the methods to overcome them.

### SEPARATING FROM BEING A PLACE HOLDER

One possibility is that a child is acting as a Place Holder—holding on to the idea that continuing the negative attitudes or behaviors avoids attention being focused on other serious issues, outside of, yet related to, the child. For example, "If I 'get better,' then Mommy and Daddy won't have to pay as much attention to me, their unhappiness and fighting will get worse, and they will get divorced." Or "If I begin behaving better in school, then the teacher won't have to spend as much time disciplining me, and I'll be expected to finish all my schoolwork—which I find totally boring."

If you think that this inhibition of acting as a Place Holder is a possibility for your child, here is a simple way for you to separate your child from being a Placer Holder, so that YOUMEE healing can take place.

AN INTENTION:

*Ask your child to say (or repeat after you) these words:*

"I am separate and unique,
whole and centered,
from those who need me."

After separating the child from being a Place Holder, it may be helpful for you and your child to repeat the YOUMEE session so that healing can take place.

## REMOVING A KARMIC PIECE

**Another possibility is that a child is carrying a Karmic Piece.** A Karmic Piece is a small portion of a Karmic Issue, which actually belongs to Earth. The child came in with a contract to carry a Piece of the Earth's Karma in order to lessen Earth's burden, so that Earth might be able to work through the Karmic Issue more easily.

Earth has now done the work of releasing all of her Karmic Issues. So, the child no longer needs to hold the Karmic Piece for Earth. But the child continues to hold the contract to hold the Piece.

If you think that this inhibition of carrying a Karmic Piece is a possibility for your child, here is a simple way for you to remove the contract to carry the Karmic Piece, so that YOUMEE healing can take place.

AN ACTION.

*Child stands.*

Starting anywhere on the CHILD's body, PARENT brushes
out CHILD's field, in a counter-clockwise brushing—
head to toe, with the Intention of brushing out whatever
Karmic Pieces show themselves.

After removing the Karmic Piece from your child, it may be helpful for you and your child to repeat the YOUMEE session so that healing can take place.

## OUTSIDE INTERFERENCE

**Another possibility is that Outside Interference is blocking and inhibiting the healing, or in a few rare cases makes behavior or attitudes even worse.**

Guidance teaches that the individual soul is the eternal part of each one of us that animates us and give us life, and that will continue on long after we are finished with our physical bodies. If this is so—if the soul is eternal and "lives on" after Earth-death—then it is logical to assume (and more and more of our young Indigo Children are telling us that this is surely true) that the soul existed and had a purposeful task before it came into Earth-body.

There are many different ideas about what an individual soul may have been doing before it came into Earth-body. Perhaps the soul was in the Heavenly realms with God, working on a specific Divine mission. Perhaps the soul had recently been in another body on this Earth. Perhaps the soul was in other forms on this Earth or elsewhere in the cosmos.

It is possible—though very rare—that the place where your child's soul was before it came into this Earth-body was a place that, itself, carries the 17 spiritual woundings. Your child's eternal soul holds the "imprint" of that place, *and* the woundings of that place. This Outside Interference means that the YOUMEES will not work for your child until the woundings *of that place* are spiritually healed.

If you think that the YOUMEES have not been helpful to your child's spiritual healing—and, especially, if after playing the YOUMEES, your child's attitudes or behaviors seem worse—and none of the other Fine Tuning suggestions have had any effect, then please e-mail us at Dosick@soulbysoul.com, or call us immediately, toll-free at 1-877-SOUL-KID, to let us know about the situation.

We will seek direction from our Spiritual Guidance, do any appropriate healings for the Outside Interference, and get back to you as soon as possible to let you know that you can play the YOUMEES again with your child—and now expect successful results.

# GraceLight

## Weaving Harmony
## for the
## Littlest Indigos

SPIRITUAL HEALING FOR INDIGO CHILDREN
FROM BIRTH TO AGE 7

# TO GAZE
## WITH
# UNDIMMED EYES

### Dwelling in the Light

Being a parent—being God's partner in bringing new life to this Earth, and being the caretaker and shepherd of a precious soul—is one of life's greatest blessings and most holy tasks.

Seeing our children—especially our children who do not yet talk, or are too young to be able to tell us what hurts—in physical, emotional, or spiritual pain is one of life's most agonizing trials. We hope, of course, that most of the time, our children will be healthy and happy. Yet since none of us was ever promised a life without hurt, we know that sometimes our children will suffer. And we, their parents, are the reluctant—and equally hurting—witnesses to their pain.

Sadly, in recent days and years, we have seen and felt the anguish of so many of our children.

We know: **Children being born now are wise and wondrous souls.** They come into this Earth still bathed in—and reflecting—the Light of the Divine. They long-retain eternal knowledge and the "secrets" from the Other Side; they hold a vision of perfection for us and for our world.

These extraordinary young ones are called the "Indigo Children."

We know that Indigo Children are extremely bright, exceptionally talented, and incredibly creative. Most of all, they know the Divine blueprint for our universe. In the face of this wildly imperfect world, they envision a world of harmony and tranquility, a world of peace and perfection. Yet our Indigo Children often seem ill-at-ease and unhappy. They seem uncomfortable living this Earth-life. They have a hard time getting along at home and school, and they often cry out or "act out" their dis-ease.

Because parents and teachers are not always aware of the uniqueness of these children, these young ones are often termed "difficult children" who "don't fit in" and "don't get along." They are often labeled: "learning disabled"; "hyper-active"; "attention deficient." And often, they are medicated. The children themselves are confused and bewildered. Why, they wonder, don't people understand? Why are we considered "strange" and "different," when it is really the rest of the world that is so out of tune with the harmonies of creation?

We know: These precious children are in deep pain and anguish from the tremendous dissonance they feel between the perfect knowing and vision they have, and the vastly imperfect world they experience everyday. **Their pain is on the spiritual, energetic level, sourced in the separation from God, and the bewilderment and anguish that results.**

## Spiritual Healing

We introduced *The 17: Spiritually Healing Children's Emotional Wounds* based on **the premise that the pain our Indigo Children are experiencing in this Earth-life is on the spiritual, energetic level, and it is there where healing must take place.** Children who have been in psychic pain, and their parents who have stood witness, were thrilled to have this process that brings healing and hope.

But from the beginning, there was one major difficulty with *The 17*. The process only works for children between the ages of seven and seventeen.

We have already learned, in the essay about *The 17*, that in order to participate in a spiritual healing process such as *The 17*, which requires active involvement, a child must be developmentally ready—both cognitively and spiritually. Children under the age of seven have not yet developed the cognitive abilities and skills to meaningfully participate in a healing session; and children under the age of seven are still connected to their parents by a "spiritual umbilical cord," and do not have the spiritual independence to act for themselves in bringing about healing.

## What About the Little Ones?

So, what about these little ones—the children who are still under the age of seven—whose Indigo-ness is vividly apparent?

These little ones are extremely bright; in their eyes are the soul-secrets of the universe. At the same time, they are extremely sensitive and reactive to the deep dissonance between their vision of perfection and the reality of this-world-as-it-is-now. Their discomfort is real; their pain and anguish is clearly visible.

Their parents report—and marvel: **The littlest Indigos continually exhibit their wisdom and their understanding.** And their parents report—and lament: Just as often, the littlest Indigos "act out" their unhappiness, discomfort, and pain at being here. In the extreme, we hear of three and four year olds who tell their parents, "I don't belong here. I don't want to be here anymore. I want to be dead." **The anguished cries of suicidal pre-schoolers is too much for any of us to bear.**

## GraceLight

The cries of our youngest children, and their parents who love them have been heard. **There is now a process of spiritual healing for our little ones.** It is called *GraceLight: Weaving Harmony for the Littlest Indigos.*

*GraceLight's* underlying premise is simple: Since a child under the age of seven is unable to act for his/her own spiritual healing, a parent, by following a specific healing "script," can now surrogate/act for a child in the healing process.

# GRACELIGHT

Weaving Harmony for the Littlest Indigos

is a spiritual healing process for Indigo Children
between birth and seven years of age—
effected for them by their parents—
that softens the pain of their separation from the Divine;
lessens their discomfort in Earth-existence;
and nourishes their vision of a world
of Oneness and perfection.

A *GraceLight* session takes no more than 15 minutes. Like *The 17*, *GraceLight* is sacred ritual. To be effective, it must be done exactly according to the instructions. So, please remember to follow the *GraceLight* script—the motions and words—exactly as given.

The *GraceLight* process works like this: First, the parent Sets Sacred Space, and then Balances with Earth's Energy. The parent then recites a specific Invocation of Intention. During this Invocation, the parent focuses on/"tunes into" his/her child's heart, and imagines the child's presence in the healing process. The parent imagines that bright White Light flows from Source—entering the parent from the top of the parent's head, through the parent's body into the parent's heart. Then, the parent imagines that White Light is flowing from his/her heart directly into the child's heart. This sets the connection among Source, parent, and child, and permits the parent to energetically speak for the child.

At the core of the process, the parent recites "Weaving the Harmony," a specific formulation that calls in/demands spiritual healing for the child.

Some may consider the language of "Weaving the Harmony" to be rather adamant and forceful. It is. A parent must invoke strong universal powers in order to activate and animate the healing.

At the conclusion of the process is The Limitation Release, if needed, and The Blessing, where the parent closes the process and wraps the child in the blessing of Light.

During the *GraceLight* healing session this is what happens: The parent—on behalf of the child—is **weaving a multitude of single strands of Light into one unified beam of Light.** Thus, the child neither need no longer: be "exploded" by the bombardment of intense rays of Light that can incinerate life and turn it to ashes; nor be bent and twisted by piercing rays of Light that can break the spirit of life; nor have to "hide away" his/her own Light, and deny the fullness of Being.

The new, whole, solid beam-strand of Light—sparkling, glittering, glimmering—becomes a prism through which the child's Divine-Light is layered, so that the child's Light can now shine as the brightness of the firmament, and thus, the child can affirm and celebrate his/her place as a part of "all that is."

THE GUIDE TO FACILITATING GRACELIGHT—which is the next section of this book—gives you step-by-step detailed instructions for facilitating a *GraceLight* healing session for your child.

## The Power of GraceLight

The mother of a four-year-old girl reported to one of our Facilitators that her daughter was always angry, always negative about almost everything, always unhappy. At pre-school, she often fought with the other children and yelled instead of speaking. At home, she often sat in the corner, staring off into space. The mother had just given birth to a new baby, and she was afraid that her four-year-old might, in some way, harm her little sister. After a *GraceLight* session, the mother reported that there was almost "instant change" in her daughter. She smiles, she laughs, and she gently holds the new baby while cooing at her.

Another mother reported that her two-year-old daughter, who is very verbal, cries a lot and seems very sad. The little one says things like: "I feel sad." And "I'm not happy here." And "Mama, make me happy." After a *GraceLight* session, the little girl is now happy and joyful, and does not speak anymore about being sad.

After seeing their little children in such pain for so long, parents call *GraceLight* a blessing.

# The Platinum Indigos

**The Platinum Indigo Children—a sub-category of Indigo Children—began coming into this Earth-life in 1964, and now, more than 60 percent of our Indigo Children are Platinums.** So, it is very likely than a very high percentage of our littlest ones are Platinums.

The Platinums need an even more powerful spiritual healing than *GraceLight* can provide because they **Carry a Memory Impact, a cellular imprint from their most recent previous lifetime.** Platinums last lifetime ended in the 1960s or the 1970s, either in a drug-induced daze or coma, or in combat in Vietnam. They bring those experiences into this lifetime and display characteristics that reflect those experiences.

Like older Indigos, these Platinums are hyper-sensitive to certain foods and environmental conditions, to emotional intensity, confusion and chaos; and they have a very low tolerance for stress and frustration. They often have learning disorders and/or comprehension and expression disorders. Since our littlest ones may not yet talk, or may have trouble finding the words to describe their discomfort, they often act out their pain in emotional and physical extremes. They often "lose it" or "melt-down."

Parents: We know that you watch in agony not knowing how to best help alleviate your young children's great anguish.

Guidance teaches that the Platinums will benefit from a special healing process called The Limitation Release. So, if you sense that your child is a Platinum Indigo, add The Limitation Release to *GraceLight* immediately following Weaving the Harmony.

Coupled with *GraceLight*, we believe that The Limitation Release will soften the overt symptoms and help bring deeper healing to our little ones who are Carrying a Memory Impact.

# Again and Again

Even with the positive and happy reports about the healing power of *GraceLight*, we need to be very clear. Most certainly, through the *GraceLight* process, children will feel relief from their spiritual pain and be more comfortable in their Earth-existence. They will have their vision of perfection affirmed and validated. Yet while *GraceLight*—even with the addition of The Limitation Release for Platinum Indigos—is a powerful and profound healing, it is not as powerful and profound as *The 17.*

It cannot be. *GraceLight* is surrogated healing, and surrogated process-es "wear off" much sooner than self-sufficient processes. And *GraceLight* is an "interim" healing, an "in the meantime" healing—a healing where the parent, in essence, says to the child: "I will hold the spiritual space for you until you are old enough to do this spiritual healing on your own." The parent—even the most loving and involved parent—acting for the child, cannot be as effective as the child acting on his/her own.

So, to be continually effective, the *GraceLight* process should be repeat-ed once each month until the child reaches age seven. Ideally, the *GraceLight* process should be done each month on—or close to—the child's date of birth. For example, if a child was born on August 6, the *GraceLight* process is best done on the sixth of each month—September 6, October 6. . . . By "coming into the Light" on his/her birthdate each month, the child affirms his/her cosmic connection and celebrates his/her unique place in the universe.

As soon as a child reaches age seven, he/she should have a *17* session, where the child fully participates in his/her own healing.

## At Stake: Sky Blue

**Every Human Being holds a vision of perfection for our world—the time of ultimate understanding and harmony, love, and peace.**
From the image of a childhood game, we call this place of perfection Sky Blue.
For some, the vision of Sky Blue has been lost in the harsh realities of this-world existence. For our little children, still "warm" from being with God, the vision is still very bright and compelling. Before their vision of perfection is dimmed by imperfections of this world—and before they suffer too much pain and anguish over the dimming of their vision—we can offer them healing and hope. Only when our children are healed and whole can the world move beyond the pain of this third dimension exis-tence into the fourth and fifth dimensions where the Divinely Sourced vision of perfection becomes Earth-reality.
Now is the time for our Littlest Indigos—who have too often been without Voice—to claim their Voice and to claim their healing. The jour-ney to Sky Blue—led by our children—begins now.

## DEAREST PARENTS

Your children chose you to be their parents for a reason. They knew that this moment would come. So, now, one of your most essential—and life-sustaining—tasks as their parents awaits.

You can bring your children—our Littlest Indigos—to the healing they so need, they so deserve. By choosing to give your children *GraceLight*, you affirm God's Grace in them, and you inflame God's Light in them. You give them the gift of being able to gaze at this universe with undimmed eyes.

As you embrace this holy task, we invite you to remember this story.

One day, a little child fell down in the snow:
The child called out, "Help me! Help me!"
The master came,
And lay down beside the child.
The child got up,
And went away.

May it be this way for you and your children.
And for our world with you.

# THE GUIDE
## TO
# GRACELIGHT

## GETTING READY

1.  When you facilitate the *GraceLight* process, you will have to concentrate deeply and focus completely, because it is not always easy acting on behalf/surrogating for another—especially your child, to whom you are so energetically connected. In addition, you will be spending time "In the Light," which takes a great deal of spiritual energy.

    So: please consider your session to be a "scheduled appointment."

    Don't be interrupted by ringing telephones or doorbells.

    Don't be distracted by your other children.

    > It is best that you make arrangements for your other children to be out of the house, or to be cared for by another, while you are facilitating *GraceLight*.

    > In this way, you will not be distracted by worrying about your other children's whereabouts or well-being, and their behavior or energy will not enter into the session.

2. It is best if the room in which you facilitate *GraceLight* is quiet, light, and airy.

3. If you have more than one child with whom you want to facilitate *GraceLight,* it may be tempting to schedule the sessions one right after the other, especially since the space is already set, you are in the Light, and you are in the healing mood and mode.

> Yet we have found that sessions that are held one after another tend to hold less success for healing.
>
> > Perhaps your energy is slightly lower in the second session.
> >
> > Perhaps some small percentage of your energy and/or attention becomes focused away from the second session.
> >
> > Perhaps something in the house, or another child's whereabouts or well-being, causes some slight distraction.
>
> Whatever the reason that back-to-back sessions are not as effective as individual sessions, we suggest that it is best to separate the *GraceLight* sessions for your two or more children by a number of hours, or, better yet, to hold the sessions on different days.

## Facilitating GraceLight

1. Please familiarize yourself with the whole *GraceLight* process by reading the entire set of instructions before you begin a *GraceLight* session for your child.

2. Please follow the processes and the "script," according to instructions, as closely as you can. Anytime the instructions ask you to "say" specific words, please say the words out loud.

BEGIN BY:
Setting Sacred Space
Performing the Energy Balance
Reciting the Invocation

THEN:
Weave the Harmony, declaration by declaration,
remembering to breathe deeply between each declaration.

IF:
You sense that your child is a Platinum Indigo who is Carrying a
Memory Impact, Recite The Limitation Release.

TO CONCLUDE THE SESSION:
Recite the Blessing
Close the Sacred Space

3.  When you complete the session, give your child a "gift" of a
    stone, or a seashell, or a little piece of driftwood—anything
    that comes directly from the natural world.

    > The energy of the Earth-element will support your
    > child's integration of the healing, allowing the healing
    > to be smoother and easier.

    > Even if your child is too young to appreciate the gift,
    > or too little to hold or have it, set the gift near the
    > child's bed, because it will provide strong balancing
    > Energy to your child.

    > Since you will be repeating *GraceLight* once each
    > month until your child reaches seven years of age,
    > your child will have a fine collection of powerful heal-
    > ing objects right at his/her side.

4.  Please remember to facilitate *GraceLight* once each month, on
    or close to your child's birthdate in each month. This is the
    way to keep the spiritual healing flowing.

5.  Please remember to schedule a *17* session as soon as your
    child reaches seven years of age in order to lock in the healings
    and make them permanent.

As you embrace this sacred task,
we thank you and we honor you
for bringing spiritual healing
to your child.

I

# SETTING SACRED SPACE

For *GraceLight* to be most effective, the room in which you do the process needs to be SACRED SPACE. When you SET SACRED SPACE, you align the energy in the room with the Earth's Energy; you invite in Divine Light; and you infuse the space with a vortex of Light Energy, that raises the space to a higher vibrational level.

Set SACRED SPACE. This is best accomplished by symbolically representing Four Elements. To do this, place symbols in the room—one in each of the four corners of the room—representing Earth's Four Elements. (It does not matter which symbol is in which corner of the room.)

1. A small bowl filled with dirt, or a piece of wood, or a rock, or a crystal, which represents the element of **Earth.**

2. A feather, or a filled balloon, which represents the element of **Air.**

3. A lamp, or a flashlight, with the lightbulb turned on, or a lighted candle, which represents the element of **Fire.**

4. A glass of water, which represents the element of **Water.**

> After you have completed the *GraceLight* process,
> please remember to close the Sacred Space
> by removing the Earth Element symbols
> from the room.

Continue with the ENERGY BALANCE.

# 2

# ENERGY BALANCE

To begin the *GraceLight* process, balance your body, mind, emotional, and spiritual energies with the Earth's Energy. Follow these steps to do the ENERGY BALANCE.

1. Plant your feet firmly on the ground.

2. Breathe deeply, inhaling and exhaling three times.

3. Cross your arms over your chest, hands at your shoulders. Breathe deeply three times.

4. Reverse your cross. Breathe deeply three times.

5. Put your hands on your lap, and say: "Light and Love."

Continue with the INVOCATION.

# 3

# INVOCATION

Take three deep breaths, inhaling and exhaling loudly, and then recite this INVOCATION.

1. Say: "We ask that the healing we are about to do be done with grace, for the highest good of all involved."

2. Focus on/"tune into" your child's heart.

    A. Imagine that your child is standing or sitting right in front of you.

    B. Imagine that dazzling, bright White Light is flowing from Above—from Source—into the top of your head and through your body into your heart.

    C. Now, imagine that the White Light is flowing from your heart directly into your child's heart.

    Please stay constantly aware of the White Light flowing from heart to heart and keep it flowing throughout the entire *GraceLight* process.

3. With your words traveling on the stream of White Light that is flowing from your heart to your child's heart, say:

    "It is my intention that my heart be tuned into my child, _____'s Heart."
    Name of child

    With the White Light flowing from heart to heart and your statement of Intention, you are now energetically able to speak/act for your child.

4. Take three deep breaths.

    Continue with WEAVING THE HARMONY.

# 4

# WEAVING THE HARMONY

Stand and recite the following three statements, one at a time, phrase-by-phrase as it is written, taking a breath after each phrase, and breathing deeply between each of the statements.

Please consider and think deeply about the words of each of the statements; let the words resonate and echo deeply within you; and let the feelings that the words spark fill your whole Being.

> "We who stand at the Precipice demand
> that all Constructs that stand in opposition to the Light
> be softened and embraced.
> > With Love and Peace.
> > With Ease and Grace."

### Breathe deeply.

> "We who stand at the Precipice demand
> that all the World heed our voices
> and stand with us in Full Consciousness.
> > With Love and Peace.
> > With Ease and Grace."

### Breathe deeply.

> "We who stand at the Precipice demand
> that all Hearts be One
> in Remembrance of Who We Are, and What Can Be.
> > With Love and Peace.
> > With Ease and Grace."

### Breathe deeply.

If you sense that your child is a PLATINUM INDIGO
who is CARRYING A MEMORY IMPACT,
go on to THE LIMITATION RELEASE.
Otherwise, go on to THE BLESSING.

# 5

# THE LIMITATION RELEASE

If you sense that your child is a **PLATINUM INDIGO** who is **CARRYING A MEMORY IMPACT,** on behalf of your child, recite this **LIMITATION RELEASE.**

"I now completely release
all limitation imposed upon my Being
by the memories I carry."

On behalf of your child: Touch your wrists together (as though your hands are in a praying position) and spread your hands apart slightly (as though your hands are in a catching position)

And say:

## Concluded, Complete, Discharged

Go on to THE BLESSING.

# 6

# THE BLESSING

After completing Weaving the Harmony, recite this BLESSING to complete the *GraceLight* process.

1. Say: "We ask that transformation be allowed in all bodies simultaneously, with Wisdom and Peace."

2. Now, imagine that the White Light that has been flowing between your heart and your child's heart is now completely taken in by your child's heart.

> With the completion of this *GraceLight* process, the White Light that has been flowing from Source to you now ends.

> All the Light that has flowed from Source through you to your child is now in your child.

3. Say: "We pray that the sacred process we are now involved with, be manifest with grace and love, for the highest good of all involved.

> And we close for now, with Love and Peace."

This concludes this *GraceLight* session.
CONGRATULATIONS to you and your child!
This would be the perfect time to give your child
the little gift of a stone, or a seashell, or a piece of driftwood.

In order to help ensure continuing spiritual health and well-being for you and for your child, please remember to close the Sacred Space.

# 7

# CLOSING SACRED SPACE

After you have completed the *GraceLight* process,
please remember to close the Sacred Space
by removing the Earth Element symbols
from the room.

Although it feels very good to "sit in the Light,"
if you stay for too long,
it is exhausting;
it takes up too much of your "soul Energy."

When you remove the symbols, you return the space
to the 3-dimensional plane,
and you reclaim YourSelf
and your full capacity
to function on this Earth plane.

Please go on to read AND NOW on the next page.

This will remind you of the need to repeat the *GraceLight* process
once each month in order to continually affirm spiritual healing
for your child.

We join your child in thanking you
for guiding this sacred process,
which brings the blessings of spiritual healing
and Divine Light and Love.

# AND NOW

## Please Remember

1. Because children younger than seven years of age cannot yet take psychic responsibility for their own spiritual healing, and because you, the parent, acted spiritually on behalf of your child, *GraceLight* is an "interim" healing.

2. In order to be effective, *GraceLight* must be repeated once a month until your child reaches the age of seven.

   > Please facilitate a *GraceLight* session for your child once each month, most preferably on or near your child's birthdate.

   > For example: If your child was born on August 6, please facilitate the *GraceLight* session on or near to the 6th of each month.

3. As soon as your child reaches age seven, please facilitate a full *17* session with your child. Following that first *17* session, please facilitate the follow-up *17* session three months after the first session. In this way, the spiritual healings for your child will be locked in and made permanent.

# The Point
## of
# Essence Process

## Pro-Claiming the Truth
## of Who You Are

SPIRITUAL HEALING FOR ADULT INDIGOS

# WHO AM I?

## Strangers in a Strange Land

Is life on this Earth painful for you?

Do you ever feel as if you do not belong here?

Do you ever feel as if you have been hiding your real Self all your life?

Do you ever have to deny your real knowing in order to "get along"?

Do you ever feel as if even those closest to you do not know the real you?

Do you think of yourself as a failure?

Do you feel as if you never experience real joy?

Do you yearn for a place that feels like "home"?

If these questions resonate within you and touch your heart and soul at their deepest places, you may be an **Adult Indigo** still **carrying**—and **suffering** from—the **emotional wounds of childhood.**

For you, life on this Earth has probably been—and continues to be—confusing and difficult.

Your inherent knowing is not acknowledged.

Your intuitive wisdom is not honored.

Your felt-sense of experience is not embraced.

Almost no one understands or appreciates you.

You try and try and try to "go along" and to "get along," but in your own eyes, almost everything you do fails.

The only way you have been able to exist in this world is to deny the essence of your Being.

Your Light has been dimmed, and your greatness has been diminished; you feel invisible and impotent.

You are cut off from your Source and your Spirit.
You are alone and lonely.
And you wonder why such a sad fate has befallen you.

## Indigo Children

You know about the Indigo Children who are born into Earth as pure Light channels of God, remembering more and more eternal knowledge, remembering more and more of the secrets from the Other Side, and holding the God-vision of a perfect world. These "old souls" have come to embody a massive paradigm shift for our entire universe and to lead us toward ever-expanding world consciousness and a perfected world.

You also know that because of their inherent wisdom, knowing, and vision, they often have a hard time getting along in this world that does not understand or appreciate their uniqueness and their special gifts. This great dissonance between their perfect knowing and their this-Earth experience causes them tremendous pain and anguish.

Parents and teachers, who do not understand the source or the cause of Indigo-pain, have sought myriad ways to help them. But the pain of Earth existence that Indigo children feel is not due to the normal vicissitudes of life and rarely responds to attempts at healing that take place on the rational, intellectual, cognitive level.

The Indigos' pain is the existential angst and loneliness that is caused by their separation and disconnection from God, by the dissonance they feel between their knowing of what a perfected world can be, and their experience of the world as it is. Their emotional pain resides on the spiritual, energetic—soul—level, and that is where their pain must be healed. That is why the spiritual healing processes, *The 17* and *GraceLight*, have been so effective for our Indigo Children.

## You

At the deepest soul level, you resonate with all the characteristics—and the emotional pain—of the Indigo Children. For while today, more than 80 percent of the children being born are Indigos, **the Indigo**

**Children first started coming into this Earth—at the rate of perhaps 5 percent–10 percent a year—right after World War II.**

You are one of those Indigos. And there were not many like you when you were young!

During your childhood, you may have had a unique perspective on life that was probably not shared by members of your family, by classmates and friends, by teachers or coaches. You "got it" far more swiftly than anyone else, and you had little patience for those who were not as quick or as bright as you. You may have felt "out of place" and wondered what you were doing here. You may have felt constantly "out of sync" with the rest of the world. You may have been one of the first to wonder why things were done in a certain way, one of the first to question authority.

Like today's Indigos, you held warm memories of being with God; you held eternal knowledge for a long, long time; you held a vision of a perfect world. On a spiritual, energetic level, you felt the pain of the dissonance between your knowing and your everyday reality. But your spiritual woundings were unrecognized and unhealed, and you have carried those spiritual woundings into adulthood.

Those unhealed spiritual woundings are a cause of your angst and anguish, the cause of your discomfort with having to function in this world, the cause of your dis-ease with being in body and being on Earth.

## Your Point of Essence

As an early Indigo, you quickly learned that the **world could not handle the full truth of who you are, the full expression of your Point of Essence.**

Your Point of Essence is the place where you are **connected to God.**

Your Point of Essence is the place of your **"I Am Presence,"** your **"GodSelf."**

Your Point of Essence is the place where ego melts away, and where **you are your unique and ultimate Self.**

Your Point of Essence is the **truth of who you are.**

Your Point of Essence is **the clearest expression of the "You-ness" of You.**

As an early Indigo, you intuitively understood that if you were to survive and function in this world, you had better hide your Essence. So, for almost all your life, you have been disconnected from your "I Am Presence," your true Self, the "You-ness of You."

## THE 7 DIS-CLAIMERS

**You learned to cope.**

Your own inner resources and the gifts of the universe combined to give you strategies and mechanisms to make your way in this world.

Without being consciously aware, you found the way to live in this world.

In order to "make it" and "get along," on a soul level, you have hidden away your true Being. You have shut down the Essence of your Being.

You have covered your Light, and shrunk from your greatness.

On a spiritual level, in seven ways, you "Dis-Claimed" the real you.

These 7 Dis-Claimers were your way of disavowing and denying your "You-ness." By embracing and adopting these 7 Dis-Claimers, you were able to function as a "stranger in a strange land."

Each of the 7 Dis-Claimers manifests in one of the body-place chakras and results in a particular blocking of the clear and open flow of Light and Love—the manifestation of the separation between you and God.

The 7 Dis-Claimers, their spiritual definitions, and their chakra places and manifestations are:

# 1. CONFUSION

**Not being clear who you are.**

Manifests in: **the 7th chakra—The top of the head**

The Channel of Divine Light is fuzzy and diffused.

# 2. SEPARATION

**Disconnection from God, and the
bewilderment and pain that results.**

SEPARATION embodies and includes all
the 17 Emotional Woundings of Childhood

Manifests in: **the 6ᵗʰ chakra—The third eye**

The place of Vision, the Gateway to memory and
Experience of the Divine, is blocked.

These are the 17 spiritual woundings and their spiritual definitions that an Adult Indigo may carry unhealed from childhood to adulthood.

1. ANGER is a need to defend oneself, through attack, against the harshness of this-world experience.

2. GRIEF is weeping at the separation.

3. FEAR is the experience of being in danger because of being too small, "too little."

4. DISTRUST is not being able to count on any reality as certain.

5. DESPAIR is giving up the connection to the breath of God.

6. ANGUISH is the belief in aloneness.

7. SHAME is being embarrassed in front of the whole cosmos.

8. INSECURITY is the experience of having no solid ground inside.

9.  SELFISHNESS is the fear of coming out to interact with this world experience.

10. LOSS is not being able to find one's own heart.

11. PANIC is the experience of being suspended in mid-air, with nothing to grasp or hold on to.

12. INFERIORITY is the belief "I'll never be as good as God."

13. HATRED is the experience of feeling as though one does not deserve re-union.

14. INDIGNATION is holding righteousness in response to the lack of dignity expressed for God's creatures.

15. RESENTMENT is the wish that the world matches the inner vision.

16. JEALOUSY is wanting what the angels have.

17. GUILT is holding oneself responsible for the lack of perfection in the world.

# 3. DISAPPEARANCE

**Hiding away. The belief of being invisible.**

Manifests in: **the 5ᵗʰ chakra—The throat**

The Voice, the place of expression, is shut down.

# 4. RESPONSIBILITY

**When hindered from the free expression of Divine Love, that Love morphs into a heavy sense of responsibility for the well-being of the world.**

Manifests in: **the 4th chakra—The heart**

The place where Infinite Love is blocked or flows freely.

# 5. NUMBNESS

**Being "dead" inside**

Manifests in: **the 3rd chakra—The solar-plexus**

The place of personal Light and Power, the center of The Life Force, is blocked, and all is ashes.

# 6. HELPLESSNESS

**Not being able to make a difference**

Manifests in: **the 2nd chakra—The intestines, the "guts," the womb**

The place of creativity is disconnected from the Infinite and from the Self.

# 7. JUDGMENT

**The verdict of failure heard from the Self and from the World.**

Manifests in: **the 1ˢᵗ chakra—The very bottom of the spine**

The place of sitting; some say it moves down toward the ankles
not having a place of safety when all is lost.

## The Point of Essence Process

There is no reason for you to be in existential angst or spiritual pain
any longer. You deserve an open, easy, comfortable, spiritual existence.

So, for you, an Adult Indigo who carried over the woundings of childhood into adulthood, we now have a spiritual healing process: *The Point of
Essence Process: Pro-Claiming the Truth of Who You Are.*

---

### The Point of Essence Process
#### Pro-Claiming the Truth of Who You Are

is spiritual healing for Adult Indigos that unblocks your lifetime's
constraints, restraints, and soul-suppressions;
reconnects the "You-ness of You" with the Divine;
affirms the full truth of your Self and the full expression
of your Being; allows you to reclaim your soul-purpose
and your soul-mission on Earth;
and helps to renew your vision of a perfect world.

---

Similar to *The 17* YOUMEE games, *The Point of Essence Process* is a series of 7 little ritual-games—7 to correspond to the 7 Dis-Claimers—played by an Adult Indigo.

These 7 ritual-games are called the 7 Pro-Clamations.

For, in engaging in these 7 spiritual, energetic level ritual-games, you replace the 7 Dis-Claimers with 7 Pro-Clamations of the truth of who you are. The Dis-Claimers—that which have been holding you back from the true expression of your "You-ness"—are superseded by the Pro-Clamations of the true essence of your Being.

You pro-claim the truth of who you are.

You joyfully reclaim your Essence, the place of your "I Am Presence," the "You-ness of You," so that you can express your full Self, the full truth of your Being, in this world.

## Sweet, Gentle Healing

A *Point of Essence* healing session takes less than an hour.

The 7 Pro-Clamations are a combination of gentle movements and the recitation of powerful statements, which work on the energetic, spiritual level. Like *The 17* and *GraceLight*, *The Point of Essence Process* is a sacred ritual. To be effective, it must be done exactly according to the instructions. So, please remember to follow *The Point of Essence* script—the motions and words—exactly as given.

You do not have to set Sacred Space because *The Point of Essence Process* uses "I Am" language where your Essence is directly connected with Source. Since you are, literally, in Sacred Space, there is no need to symbolically represent it. In the same way, there are no male-female differentiations in words or actions during *The Point of Essence Process*. Since the "I Am" language puts you in direct connection with Source, and since in Source there is complete Wholeness and Oneness, there is no need make any accommodation for any this-Earth gender differences.

The Pro-Clamations are preceded by a simple Energy Balance and the recitation of an Intention.

If needed, The Redemption Process is recited during Pro-Clamation #2. The Pro-Clamations are followed by a Blessing and a Seal, affirming and "locking in" the spiritual work that has just been done.

THE GUIDE TO FACILITATING THE POINT OF ESSENCE PROCESS—which is the next section of this book—gives you step-by-step detailed instructions for facilitating a *Point of Essence Process* for yourself.

## Adult Platinum Indigos

**Platinum Indigos began to come into this Earth-life in 1964.** They are a special sub-category of Indigos whose most recent previous lifetime, in the 1960s or the 1970s, ended in a drug-induced daze or coma, or in combat in Vietnam.

In this lifetime, they are **Carrying a Memory Impact** from the last lifetime, and they often bring with them into this lifetime the characteristics that reflect that previous lifetime. **It is imprinted at the cellular level, which can affect them even on a physiological level in this lifetime.**

The result is a high possibility of hyper-sensitivity to emotional chaos, confusion, environmental factors, and certain foods, and a low tolerance for stress or frustration. There is also the high likelihood of learning disorders and/or comprehension and expression disorders.

If you are of the right age and some of these symptoms resonate with you, it is possible that you are an Adult Platinum Indigo, having carried over your unhealed Platinum Indigo-ness from childhood to adulthood. For you, there is a special healing called The Redemption Process.

If you sense that you are an Adult Platinum Indigo, add The Redemption Process to *The Point of Essence Process* during Pro-Clamation #2, Separation. Dis-Claimer #2, Separation, includes and embodies all the 17 emotional woundings of childhood, so it is the prefect place for The Redemption Process, which serves to bring spiritual healing to the wounds of childhood.

We believe that The Redemption Process, coupled with *The Point of Essence Process*, will soften the overt symptoms and help bring deeper healing to your Platinum Indigo-ness.

Our sense is that *The Point of Essence Process*—especially with the addition of The Redemption Process for Platinum Indigos—is a very, very powerful healing technique. And our sense is that it is helpful for every Adult Indigo. But there may be other issues keeping you from expressing the fullness of your Being. These, for example, may be karmic issues, life-patterns, field-attachments, Energetic interference, or past life bleed-through.

These issues will probably not respond to *The Point of Essence Process,* and most probably will require other types of healing to be resolved—most notably and effectively, Soul Memory Discovery.[3]

Some Adult Indigos may be deeply affected and healed by one *Point of Essence* session. Others, perhaps up to 60 percent—for whom the 7 Dis-Claimers are so embedded and have so forcefully mapped and driven the coping mechanisms of a lifetime—one session may not suffice. Based on your sense of your unfolding progression in reclaiming your truth and your "You-ness," you will determine your own need and desire for additional sessions.

Simply: Listen to your truth. It will guide you.

---

### DRAGONFLIES

Guidance teaches:

There is a group of people, born between 1947 and 1957, at the rate of 5 percent. If you are part of this group, you feel, but you don't remember. That means that you resonate with many of the characteristics of the Indigos, but that you are not an Indigo. You do not hold the eternal memory and the world-vision that Indigos carry. You also do not carry the spiritual woundings of Adult Indigos, so you do not need *The Point of Essence Process.*

Instead, you have a unique role and a unique designation. You were born for the very special purpose of birthing Indigos, recognizing who they are and supporting them in their evolution. You are called a **Dragonfly.** And because, in many ways, you identify and feel with Indigos at the soul level, you are an incredible blessing to the Indigo Children you mother or father on this Earth.

---

[3] For a full description of the principles and process of Soul Memory Discovery, please see Accompaniment II, "Explaining Soul Memory Discovery" at the back of this book.

## Opening the Flow

Unlike *The 17* for children, *The Point of Essence Process* does not usually produce swift, dramatic results. Rather, it initiates a gradual, but eventually, forceful and profound opening. Restraints and blocks of a lifetime begin to dissipate. Fuzzy channels are "unfuzzed." The flow begins.

Take, for example, a man who lives in another state who came for a *Point of Essence* session. In the weeks following the session, we did not hear from him; he did not report about the results of the session. A few months later, we saw him at a social gathering here in San Diego. He said, "I didn't get in touch with you after my *Point of Essence* session, because it really didn't do anything for me; nothing really changed. And since I like you and didn't want to hurt your feelings, I didn't want to let you know that the process didn't work."

After the "socially proper" exchange about his reaction to *The Point of Essence*, we asked, "What are you doing here in San Diego again?" He replied, "Didn't you hear? Since I last saw you, I sold my business back home and rented out my house. I've moved here, and since I've been here, I rented an apartment, started a new business, and have a new girlfriend."

We looked at him with amazement. "And *The Point of Essence* session didn't work?"

"You know," he said, "I never thought of it that way. I guess that you were right. You said that the opening might be gradual, and it was, so I never attributed any of this to the session." And he smiled a great big smile. And the next day, he called to schedule another appointment.

Yet sometimes, the opening is very quick and very powerful.

A woman in her early 50s came to one of our Facilitators for a *Point of Essence Process* session. The woman, who is black and Puerto Rican, lives and works in a "lily white" community where she teaches languages at the local high school. She is the divorced mother of a teen-age son who lives with his father in a town about two hours away.

She is a self-described "late bloomer" who has felt "separate" all her life and now is filled with self-doubt about her success as a teacher and her job as a mother. At school, she feels as if she is an "outsider," because of her race, and her skills as a Spanish teacher (a skill that is not highly valued in that community), and her lack of social contact with the other teachers. At home, she feels inadequate because she sees her son only on weekend visits, and so, she thinks that because she is not his full-time mother, that she is "losing him."

She would like her life to be different, but she feels "stagnant" and unable to change. She lacks the self-confidence to think that change is possible, or even that she deserves better than she has. When she considered buying a new house, she wondered, "Why would a poor girl like me think that she can buy this kind of nice place?"

Immediately following her *Point of Essence Process* session, she decided to apply for a new job in a community closer to where her son lives with his father. Even though budgets are tight and new hiring was supposedly on hold at the time, she was hired immediately—at a salary more than 30 percent higher than at her current job. In this primarily Hispanic school district, she fits right into the ethnic make-up of the school, and her skills as a bi-lingual teacher are highly valued.

She bought a house in the new community worth far more than the house she was selling, because, with her higher salary, she qualified for a better mortgage. She clearly and bravely articulated her needs to the realtor and the loan officers, and the loan process and the closing on the house went smoothly and swiftly. She now proudly has the kind of house she once thought she would "never deserve."

She decided to ask for what she really wanted. She asked her son if he would like to live with her. The son said "yes," and the father readily agreed. Now, mother and son are living together again, and she is the full-time mom she always wanted to be.

When asked why she thought all these positive changes had come to her life so quickly, she replied, "I don't know. I just decided to 'go for it.' I finally stood up for myself and get what I really want."

"And," we asked, "what about *The Point of Essence Process*?"

She smiled and said, "All this began happening to me right after the session. Thank you, *Point of Essence Process*."

*The Point of Essence Process* session
pro-claims the real you,
celebrates the real you,
and can lead to profound life-evolution,
and stirring soul-transformation.

## At Stake: Sky Blue

Over the years and the decades, your vision and the expression of the truth of your vision may have been blurred. But *The Point of Essence Process: Pro-Claiming the Truth of Who You Are* reclaims and renews that vision for you.

And that vision becomes as clear and as strong and as urgent for you as it is for our children. For they and you envision a perfect world—a place where, beyond the limitations of the present time and space, there is an end to hatred and bigotry, warfare and violence; a time and place of reconciliation and healing, transformation and transcendence; a time and place of decency and dignity, justice and compassion, goodwill and gladness, harmony and peace, faith and love—the vision of that world, "Sky Blue."

"Sky Blue" is the very best place you can be—the pinnacle of perfection.

The only way to reach Sky Blue is to bring healing to our children and to ourselves—one by one, soul by precious soul—so that our world can move dimensions and enter a higher vibrational level.

Then—and only then—can we reach that best-of-all moments when joyful tranquility will envelop the universe, when there will be peace in every home and love in every heart.

The world is ready for you now.
The world needs you and your vision now.
So, we invite you to healing.
We invite you to finally be able to embrace the truth
and the fullness of your Being.
We invite you to journey toward Sky Blue.

## Dear Ones

It is told: A handful of wheat,
five thousand years old,
was found in the tomb of one of the kings of ancient Egypt.
Someone planted the grains,
and to the amazement of all,
the grains came to life.

The Essence of your life-force has been buried and hidden away for all these years.

But what has been lost is now found.

"What lies behind us and what lies before us are tiny matters compared to what lies within us."

The Essence of Your Being—your Point of Essence—is now yours to plant and tend and grow.

The bountiful harvest of your life—and your world—awaits.

Plant in joy.
Reap in blessing.

# THE GUIDE
## TO THE
# POINT OF
# ESSENCE PROCESS

### GETTING READY

1.  To facilitate a *Point of Essence* session for yourself, it will be easiest if you have a spouse or partner or friend help you conduct the healing session, because it can be difficult to serve as both facilitator and participant at the same time. Yet if no one else is available to help you, please feel enabled and empowered to do the session by yourself.

2.  When you facilitate a *Point of Essence* session for yourself, please consider your session to be a "scheduled appointment." Don't be interrupted by other people in the house, or by ringing telephones, or doorbells.

3.  It is best if the room in which you facilitate the session is quiet, light, and airy. Give yourself the optimum conditions in which to do this sacred work.

4.  You will need a chair in which to sit to make some of the Pro-Clamations.

## FACILITATING THE POINT OF ESSENCE PROCESS

1. Please familiarize yourself with the whole *Point of Essence Process* by reading the entire set of instructions before you begin a session.

2. Please follow the processes and the "script," according to instructions, as closely as you can. Remember: Unlike *The 17* and *GraceLight* for your children, you do not have to Set Sacred Space for the *Point of Essence* session, because the "I Am" language of the process puts you directly into Sacred Space without the need to symbolically represent it.

   Anytime the instructions ask you to "say" specific words, please say the words out loud.

BEGIN BY:
Performing the Energy Balance, and
Reciting the Intention.

THEN:
Make Pro-Clamations, 1 and 2, step-by-step,
following the numbered instructions.

As you recite each Pro-Clamation, say it phrase-by-phrase,
as it is written, taking a breath between each phrase.

During Dis-Claimer and Pro-Clamation #2—
which embodies all 17 spiritual woundings
that you have carried from childhood to adulthood—

IF:
You sense that you are an Adult Platinum Indigo who is
Carrying a Memory Impact, please follow the instructions
to recite The Redemption Process.

IF YOU ARE NOT a Platinum Indigo,
please simply follow the instructions
to conclude Pro-Clamation #2.

Either way, then continue on to make each Pro-Clamation,
3 through 7, step-by-step,
following the numbered instructions.

TO CONCLUDE THE SESSION:
Recite the Blessing, and Recite the Seal.

3.  When you complete the session, you may want to give your-
    self a little "gift" of a stone, or a seashell, or a little piece of
    driftwood—anything that comes directly from the natural
    world. The energy of the Earth-element will support your
    integration of the healing, allowing the healing to be
    smoother and easier.

4.  Read the section, And Now, on page 222, which will advise
    you about "checking-in" with your knowing to determine if
    you want further *Point of Essence* sessions.

As you embrace this sacred task,
we thank you and we honor you
for giving yourself
the gift of spiritual healing.

# I

# ENERGY BALANCE

To begin *The Point of Essence Process*, balance your body, mind, emotional, and spiritual energies with the Earth's Energy.

Follow these steps to do the ENERGY BALANCE.

1.  Plant your feet firmly on the ground.

2.  Breathe deeply, inhaling and exhaling three times.

3.  Cross your arms over your chest, hands at your shoulders. Breathe deeply three times.

4.  Reverse the cross. Breathe deeply three times.

5.  Lower your arms. Put your hands in your lap.

Continue with the INTENTION.

# 2

# INTENTION

Take three deep breaths, inhaling and exhaling loudly, and then recite this INTENTION.

"With wisdom and peace."

Go on to MAKING THE PRO-CLAMATIONS.

# 3

# MAKING
# THE PRO-CLAMATIONS

Consider each Dis-Claimer and make its corresponding Pro-Clamation in consecutive order, 1 through 7.

1.  As you come to each Dis-Claimer, spend a few moments meditating on its definition and how it resonates within you. Try to get in touch with how making this Dis-Claimer has felt to you throughout your life.

2.  Then, spend a few moments meditating on the chakra, the "power center," and its place in the physical body where the Dis-Claimer manifests. Try to get in touch with how that physical place in your body feels to you.

3.  As you make each Pro-Clamation, follow the step-by-step instructions, and please follow each script-direction exactly as it is given.

4.  If you sense that you are an Adult Platinum Indigo who is Carrying a Memory Impact, while making Pro-Clamation #2, please follow the instructions to recite The Redemption Process.

When you have completed making all the Pro-Clamations,
please be sure to turn to page 220 for
THE BLESSING
and then THE SEAL
in order to lock in the healings
and close the session.

Go on to DIS-CLAIMER AND PRO-CLAMATION 1.

### ◆ Dis-Claimer I ◆

# CONFUSION

## NOT BEING CLEAR WHO YOU ARE

Confusion manifests in **the 7th chakra—the top of the head.**

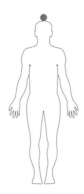

The Channel of Divine Light is fuzzy and diffused.

## PRO-CLAMATION

1. Stand with your hands at your sides, palms facing forward,

And say:

> "I Am Clear and Free
> to be Me in This World."

2. Raise your arms out to shoulder height, palms facing forward,

and spin clockwise, one time.

3. Lower your arms to your sides, palms facing forward,

And say:

> "I Am Here,
> Ready To Be the Clearest Expression
> of My Essence."

4. Raise your arms to shoulder height, palms facing forward, and spin counterclockwise, one time.

5. Lower your arms to your sides.

6. Breathe deeply.

Go on to DIS-CLAIMER AND PRO-CLAMATION 2.

## ◆ Dɪs-Cʟᴀɪᴍᴇʀ 2 ◆

# SEPARATION

### DISCONNECTION FROM GOD,
### AND THE BEWILDERMENT AND PAIN THAT RESULTS

Separation

Embodies and includes all
the 17 emotional woundings of childhood

1. ANGER is a need to defend oneself, through attack, against the harshness of this-world experience.

2. GRIEF is weeping at the separation.

3. FEAR is the experience of being in danger because of being too small, "too little."

4. DISTRUST is not being able to count on any reality as certain.

5. DESPAIR is giving up the connection to the breath of God.

6. ANGUISH is the belief in aloneness.

7. SHAME is being embarrassed in front of the whole cosmos.

8. INSECURITY is the experience of having no solid ground inside.

9. SELFISHNESS is the fear of coming out to interact with this-world experience.

10. LOSS is not being able to find one's own heart.

11. PANIC is the experience of being suspended in mid-air with nothing to grasp or hold on to.

12. INFERIORITY is the belief "I'll never be as good as God."

13. HATRED is the experience of feeling as though one does not deserve re-union.

14. INDIGNATION is holding righteousness in response to the lack of dignity expressed for God's creatures.

15. RESENTMENT is the wish that the world matches the inner vision.

16. JEALOUSY is wanting what the angels have.

17. GUILT is holding oneself responsible for the lack of perfection in the world.

SEPARATION manifests in the **6th chakra—the third eye.**

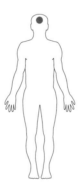

The place of Vision, the Gateway to memory and experience of the Divine, is blocked.

# PRO-CLAMATION

1.  Sit, and touch your thumb tip to your ring finger tip on both your hands,

> And say:
>
>> "I Am in Full Connection with All That Is"
>>
>> "I Am Abundant in Love"
>>
>> "I Am Wholly Aligned with Light and Blessing"

2.  Open your hands, and place them over your heart; right hand first, left hand on top of right, for as long as it feels right and good.

3.  Lower your hands; place them on your lap.

4.  If you do not feel that you are an Adult Platinum Indigo, then conclude this Pro-Clamation now by: Breathing deeply.

Go on to DIS-CLAIMER AND PRO-CLAMATION 3.

IF you sense that you are an ADULT PLATINUM INDIGO
Who is CARRYING A MEMORY IMPACT,
Please recite:

## The Redemption Process

Say: "I Am flowing with well-being."

**Breathe deeply.**

"I Am experiencing life."

**Breathe deeply.**

"I Am renewing what has been hindering."

**Breathe deeply.**

"I Am manifesting balance."

**Breathe deeply.**

"I Am becoming the flowering of Humankind."

**Breathe deeply three times.**

Go on to DIS-CLAIMER AND PRO-CLAMATION 3.

◆ Dis-Claimer 3 ◆

# DISAPPEARANCE

### HIDING AWAY;
### THE BELIEF OF BEING INVISIBLE

Disappearance manifests in the 5<sup>th</sup> **chakra—the throat.**

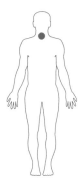

The Voice, the place of expression, is shut down.

## PRO-CLAMATION

1. Sit straight up, feet apart and planted firmly on the ground.

2. Put your arms out in front of you at shoulder height, palms facing up, at a 45 degree angle,

And say:

"I Am Here"

"I Am Safe"

"I Am Honored"

"I Am Loved"

3. Lower your arms.

4. Stand, feet apart at shoulder width.

Bend from your waist, and with your hands touching your body, sweep all the way up from your toes, up the body, and over your head.

 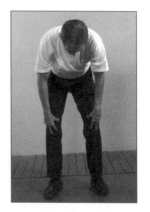

5. Hold your raised hands over your head,

And say:

"I Am Present"

"I Am Powerful"

"I Am Filled with the Light of the Divine"

6. Lower your hands/arms to your sides.

7. Breathe deeply.

Go on to DIS-CLAIMER AND PRO-CLAMATION 4.

◆ Dɪs-Cʟᴀɪᴍᴇʀ 4 ◆

# RESPONSIBILITY

WHEN HINDERED FROM THE FREE EXPRESSION
OF DIVINE LOVE,
THAT LOVE MORPHS INTO A HEAVY SENSE
OF OBLIGATION FOR THE WELL-BEING OF THE WORLD

Responsibility manifests in the **4ᵗʰ chakra—the heart.**

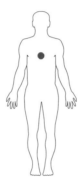

The place where Infinite Love is blocked or flows freely.

# PRO-CLAMATION

1. Sit on the floor, with your legs out in front of you, slightly apart, your hands covering your knees,

   And say:

   > "I Am in the Right Place"
   >
   > "I Am in the Right Time"
   >
   > "All is Well"

2. Sit on a chair with your legs slightly apart, your feet firmly planted on the ground, your hands at your solar-plexis (between waist and rib cage), fingers interlocking in the middle,

And say:

> "I Am Surrounded by a Universe, unfolding
> in a Perfect Order"
>
> "I Am a Universe, unfolding in a Perfect Order"
>
> "All is Well"

3.  Stand, with your legs at shoulder-width, your hands at your thymus (between throat and heart), fingers interlocking in the middle,

And say:

> "I Am at One with the Flow"
>
> "All is Well"

4.  Lower your hands/arms to your sides.

5.  Breathe deeply.

Go on to DIS-CLAIMER AND PRO-CLAMATION 5.

# ◆ Dis-Claimer 5 ◆

# NUMBNESS

### BEING "DEAD" INSIDE

**Numbness manifests in the 3rd chakra—the solar-plexis.**

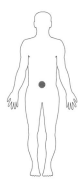

The place of personal Light and Power,
the center of life force, is blocked,
and all is ashes.

## PRO-CLAMATION

1.  Sit with your hands on your lap, and say:

    "I Am Becoming My Own Partner."

2.  Stand, with your hands at your second chakra (just below belly-button), right hand first, left hand covering right hand,

And say:

"I Am in Awe of Who I Am."

3.  Still standing, move your hands up to your face, and holding your hands vertically (fingers pointing upward), place your right hand on your forehead at your Third Eye, then place your left hand over your right hand (with bottom of hands "resting" on the bridge of your nose),

And say:

"I Am Present Within"

"I Am Alive"

4.   Lower your hands/arms to your sides.

5.   Breathe deeply.

Go on to DIS-CLAIMER AND PRO-CLAMATION 6.

# ◆ Dis-Claimer 6 ◆

# HELPLESSNESS

## NOT BEING ABLE TO MAKE A DIFFERENCE

Helplessness manifests in the **2ⁿᵈ chakra—
the intestines, the "guts," the womb.**

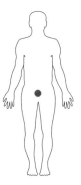

The place of creativity is disconnected
from the Infinite and from the Self.

# PRO-CLAMATION

1.  Sitting, cross your arms across your chest, as though in a stubborn or angry gesture,

  And say:

   "I Am All That I Have"

   "I Am One with All That I Have"

   "I Am All"

2.  Stand and fling your arms to your sides at shoulder height,

And say:

"I Am One—

Connected

Whole

Integrated

Powerful"

3.  Lower your arms to your sides.

4.  Breathe deeply.

Go on to DIS-CLAIMER AND PRO-CLAMATION 7.

## ◆ Dis-Claimer 7 ◆

# JUDGMENT

### VERDICT OF FAILURE HEARD FROM THE SELF AND THE WORLD

Judgment manifests in the **1ˢᵗ chakra—the very bottom of the spine—**
the place of sitting; some say it moves down toward the ankles.

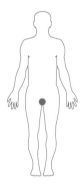

Not having a place of safety when all is lost.

## PRO-CLAMATION

1.  Sit with only your toes touching the ground (like on tippy-toe), your hands on your lap,

> And say:
>> "I Am Love."

2.  Continue sitting with only your toes on the ground (tippy-toe), and put your hands into a prayer position. Touch your index finger and your pinky finger of both hands together (index to index; pinky to pinky),

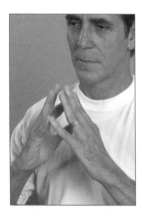

And say:

> "I Am Open
>
> and Embracing the Flow of Divine Design"
>
> "I Am Clear
>
> and Discerning the Worth of the Heart"

3.  Place your feet firmly on the ground, hold your hands together at heart level, in a prayer position—all fingers touching,

    And say:

    > "I Am Fully Returned
    >
    > as at The Very Beginning"

4.  Lower your hands/arms and place them on your lap.

5.  Breathe deeply.

Continue with THE BLESSING.

# 4

# THE BLESSING

When you have completed all 7 Pro-Clamations,
recite this BLESSING.

"I pray
that the sacred Process
I am now involved with
be manifest
with grace and love,
for the highest good,
of all involved."

Continue with THE SEAL.

# 5

# THE SEAL

To lock in and seal the Pro-Clamations, recite this SEAL.

**"Thank You, Source.
Thank You, Source.
Thank You, Source."**

This concludes *The Point of Essence Process.*
CONGRATULATIONS!
This would be the perfect time to give yourself
the little gift of a stone, or a seashell, or a piece of driftwood.

---

We honor you and celebrate you
for giving yourself the gift
of this sacred "I Am" process,
which brings the blessings of spiritual healing
and Divine Light and Love.

---

Please go on to read AND NOW on the next page.

# AND NOW

*The Point of Essence Process* reconnects you to your Essence, to the "You-ness" of You. It helps you reclaim your soul-purpose and renew your vision of perfection.

Sometimes, the process works very swiftly. The channel that has been clogged and fuzzy opens, and a torrent of healing, reconnection, and Self immediately rushes through it. Sometimes, just a trickle begins flowing through the open channel, and it takes a while for the currents of reclamation to rush through. Either way, it will be joyous, and humbling—sometimes, a little scary—and surely, life-enhancing and enriching to come into the fullness of your Being.

Do you need another *Point of Essence Process* session?

Sometimes, there are other issues that are still in your way and need to be healed by a process other than *The Point of Essence*—most notably, the most effective process we have found, Soul Memory Discovery.[4]

But based on your sense of your unfolding progression in reclaiming your truth and your "You-ness," you will determine your own need and desire for additional *Point of Essence* sessions.

Listen to your own truth.<br>
It will guide you.

---

[4] For a full description of the principles and process of Soul Memory Discovery, please see Accompaniment II, "Explaining Soul Memory Discovery," at the back of this book.

# End
# Pieces

# UPDATES

All the information in this book about the principles and processes of *The 17*, *GraceLight*, and *The Point of Essence Process* is full and complete, as we have been given it by our Spiritual Guidance.

Yet nothing ever remains the same.

Change is inevitable—in the Heavenly realms and on Earth.

As Earth and Humankind evolve, so must spiritual processes.

So, from time to time, Spiritual Guidance may give us new information to "fine tune" these Indigo spiritual healing processes.

So that you can be completely up-to-date on any new developments in these processes, we will post any new information that we receive from Guidance on our Websites:

## www.healingtheindigo.com
## www.soulbysoul.com

Click on "Updates," where you will find the most current teachings about *The 17*, *GraceLight*, and *The Point of Essence Process.*

**If you have any questions or concerns, please e-mail us at**
**Dosick@soulbysoul.com.**
**Or call us toll free at**
**1-877-SOUL-KID.**

We're here to help.

# PLEASE LET US KNOW

After you have facilitated *GraceLight* for your young one, or played the YOUMEES with your child, or facilitated *The Point of Essence Process* for yourself, please consider telling us your story. Send us a letter in care of the publisher of this book, or send us an e-mail at **Dosick@soulbysoul.com.** When we visit your city, please come to tell us your story in person. We'd love to share in your journey of healing and hope.

We respectfully ask, too, that you tell your family, friends, and neighbors, your child's teachers, instructors, coaches, and classmates' parents, the folks in your church, synagogue, mosque, or temple, the folks in your clubs and organizations, your business associates and colleagues—anybody and everybody—about this book.

In these increasingly confusing and dangerous times, our Indigo Children and our Adult Indigos—who carry the vision of perfection—feel pain and anguish more than ever before. We desperately need the spiritual healing that will bring comfort, and help show us the way toward evolution and transformation for our world.

When you recommend this book and these processes to others, you help bring spiritual healing to more and more Indigo Children and Adult Indigos, and you help bring our world one step closer to ultimate perfection.

# SEEKING FACILITATORS

We are always seeking more people to join our Network of Soul Center Facilitators.

If you have a passionate love for children and their well-being and would like to devote some of your professional or volunteer time and energy to their healing, evolution, and transformation, please consider taking our Training.

You can be the one to bring the facilitated spiritual healings of *The 17, GraceLight,* and *The Point of Essence Process* to your community.

For detailed information about the Training
and upcoming Training dates,
Check The Soul Center for Spiritual Healing Website:

## www.healingtheindigo.com
## www.soulbysoul.com

# THE CRYSTAL CHILDREN

**A new kind of child—a child beyond Indigo—is now being born into this Earth.** Just as the very first Indigos began coming to Earth—beginning some 60 years ago—at the rate of about 5 percent per year, a new child is beginning to come to Earth at the rate of about 3–5 percent a year.

These children are characterized by being pure Love.

They come with no karma, with no past life woundings.

Their faces continually glow with the Light of the Divine.

Their entire Beings are soft and gentle.

They exude an incredible sweetness.

They seem untouched by the harshness of the world, protected and shielded from the vicissitudes of life.

They are incapable of taking in anything that is not the pure Love vibration.

They come to be the realization of what the Indigo Children model for us—Beings of pure Light and Love, paradigms of a world of perfection, the living embodiment of what every Human Being on Earth can and will be.

Their aura of pure goodness lingers with us, and gives us enduring hope.

They are called "The Crystal Children," or simply, "The Crystals."

We rejoice in their presence amongst us.

We honor their purpose and their vision.

We joyfully anticipate the time when their mission will be embraced by the whole world, when The Crystal Children—cheered on by their Indigo predecessors—will lead us to the evolution and transformation that brings Eden to Earth.

# Accompaniment

## I

# THE DISCOVERY OF SPIRITUAL HEALING FOR THE INDIGOS

## In the Beginning

We have both worked with children all our lives.

Ellen has taught and counseled children and their parents at every level, directed after-school and summer programs, and directed Children's Community Theater. Wayne has taught youngsters from pre-school through graduate school, counseled at summer camps, directed day and supplementary schools and youth programs, and conducted seminars and retreats for children of all ages and their parents.

Wayne's book, *Golden Rules: The Ten Ethical Values Parents Need To Teach Their Children* (HarperCollins, 1995 and 1998), won international acclaim and has been hailed as "the best parenting manual we have ever seen" (*Minneapolis Star-Tribune*). His lectures and workshops draw crowds of parents eager for guidance in how to bring up ethical children in unethical times.

Yet back in late 1995, except for Wayne's university teaching, neither of us was directly involved in day-to-day working with children or young people.

Then, our Spiritual Guidance called.

# GUIDANCE REVEALS

At that time, Ellen, who had spent decades in practice as a "traditional" psychotherapist, was in the midst of evolving a highly spiritual psychotherapy that she calls "Soul Memory Discovery."

Soul Memory Discovery taps into a person's own eternal memory to find the originating source of a troubling issue and clear it away, so that healing takes place. Sometimes, during a Soul Memory session, a person's Guides and MasterGuides channel through to deliver messages about life purposes, about what is happening in our world, and about the missions we are to undertake in order to support the evolution of our cosmos.

During the fall of 1995, in a number of different sessions, Ellen began hearing disturbing, and what she felt to be, rather ominous information. Guidance warned that a time was coming very, very soon when "children will be in more pain than they have ever experienced before." Guidance told of children who are clear, pure channels of Light who will suffer tremendous anguish in a world that is anything but clear and pure.

They are children who hold of vision of perfection for our world, who will suffer tremendous angst in a world that constantly blurs the vision in wild imperfection. Guidance warned that the children would be in so much emotional pain they would "act out" their pain by harming others—and even themselves.

Guidance taught that our children's anguish is sourced in their bewilderment and pain at their separation from God and resides in their spiritual, emotional, energetic bodies.

Guidance told us that serious attention must be paid to the millions of children of the world who would be in deep emotional pain.

So, Guidance told us to play little games to play with children and their parents that use words and movements to act on the spiritual—the soul—level in order to bring healing to their spiritual woundings.

We learned that there are seventeen spiritual woundings that children can experience, and seventeen corresponding healing games to play. So, we called the processes *The 17*. But at that time, we only channeled four or five of the games, gave them to a few folks to try out with their children, and truth be told, we went on to other projects in our otherwise busy lives.

## Guidance Insists

Then, our house burned to the ground.

In October 1996, a Southern California wildfire destroyed our house, along with more than 100 other houses in our neighborhood. Since we both work at home, we lost everything of our personal and our professional lives. We stood in the ashes of our house, left with nothing except the clothes we had been wearing.

Most fortuitously (there are no coincidences, are there?), just a few weeks before the fire, Ellen had given her notes with the channeled games to a mother who wanted to try them with her daughter. God and the universe have funny ways of reminding us to do the work we are destined to do. The information that had been given to us about spiritual healing for our children was saved from destruction.

Some weeks after the fire, the woman who had Ellen's healing-game notes gave them back to us. We were glad to have them preserved, but in the moment-to-moment challenge of trying to make order out of the chaos of our lives, the notes just sat in a pile of papers that we would get around to looking at "some day."

## Guidance Guides

"Some day" came in the summer of 1998.

Around that time, in our prayers and meditations, we both began to hear the words: "The children. The children." We already knew that our children are very special Beings with very special gifts. Since they carry within them the vision of perfection for themselves, for us, and for our world, we thought that perhaps, we were being reminded that the world cannot come into a place of transformation and perfection—that the forces of Light cannot prevail over the forces of darkness—unless the children lead us. And we knew that until the children are healed from their emotional, spiritual pain, they cannot come into the fullness of their Being.

So, we said to each other: "Maybe we ought to take a look at those notes from the healing-games. Maybe there is something that we are supposed to be doing for the children that will be helpful to them and to the world." We dug out the notes from their pile, and we read them. We were both hit with the sense that we were holding something of high and profound purpose.

So, we called an "Ellen and Wayne Retreat." We chose two days on the calendar on which we would make no appointments and take no phone calls, and instead, we would spend our time channeling from our Spiritual Guidance all the information about the healing games for children.

We worked very hard during those two days, because Guidance was very, very specific—demanding that every single word of the information and instructions be absolutely precise. It often took quite a long time to discern exactly what word or phrase Guidance was giving.

At the same time, we felt as if we were existing in super-sacred time and space. It felt as if we were being given a glimpse of the holy. We were permitted to see—if only for a few moments—the majesty of our children's vision and the magnitude of their soul-mission on Earth.

By the end of our "Retreat," we had learned of all 17 spiritual woundings that our children, ages seven to seventeen, can carry, and of all 17 games that children and their parents can play to bring spiritual healing.

## Testing, Testing

So, we called all of our friends who have children and we said, "Please bring your children to work with us on a little research project we are doing." During the summer and early fall of 1998, we played the healing games with about 40 children and their parents.

We began to call the games YOUMEES, because they are played between "you" and "me," the child and the parent. The name caught on, and kids in the neighborhood began to call us "The YOUMEE People."

Most of the parents who played the games with their children reported that within only a few weeks, they saw dramatic changes in their children's attitudes and behaviors after playing the YOUMEES. Yet there were a few parents who reported no changes in their children after playing the YOUMEES.

We were mystified. We didn't understand why some children were so profoundly changed by the YOUMEES, while others seemed to be totally unaffected. Given our academic training, we felt that these anecdotal reports were encouraging but that we should do research with a much larger sampling of children before we announced any results. We considered seeking a grant to do research with a much larger population of children and parents.

So, we went to some of our colleagues in the academic and scientific communities and said, "Please help us devise testing and measurement instruments, and help us apply for grants to do this research." All of our colleagues replied in essentially the same way. "This is a visionary idea. It will probably help millions of children. It could very well change the world. But we can't associate our names and reputations with this program. We'll be laughed out of the scientific community."

Ah. What if Thomas Edison, and Alexander Graham Bell, and Wilbur and Orville Wright felt the need to seek scientific research grants? Where would the world be?

Even as we wondered how we could obtain the data that would give credence to the work, the continuing positive results seemed to speak for themselves. As word of what we were doing spread, people began calling to ask if their children could play the YOUMEES, too. More and more frequently, we heard the same report: When children play the YOUMEES, their emotional pain and spiritual angst seem to diminish, and their lives seem more comfortable and happy.

## They Are The Indigos

Soon, a number of people began saying to us: "I hear that you are working with the Indigo Children." "I hear that you have a spiritual healing process for the Indigo Children."

To tell you the truth, we had never heard the term "Indigo Children." So, we began to inquire. We read the literature and books about the Indigo Children, although not much was available at that time.

Fortuitously (there are no coincidences, are there?), many of the people who were teaching about and working with the Indigo Children—many of the pioneers in the field, including Nancy Ann Tappe, Lee Carroll, Jan Tober, and Dr. Doreen Virtue—are right here in Southern California where we live. We were able to talk with them and learn about their work.

We saw that most of the children with whom we were playing the YOUMEES are, indeed, Indigo Children, holding all the presently-known characteristics of Indigos—the gifts and vision, as well as the angst and anguish. We came to understand that it was these Indigo Children whom

Guidance had identified in 1995 as the children who would be in more pain than any children have ever experienced. We realized that the YOUMEES are designed specifically to help heal the spiritual woundings of the Indigos.

That is why *The 17* process does not work for some children—they are not Indigos, and the YOUMEES will not affect them.

We greatly respected and honored all the valuable work that had been done for the Indigos up until that time, and we felt that the YOUMEE games could be a worthy addition to the world of Indigos. For we sensed that what Guidance had given us was the first—if not the only—*spiritual* healing for the emotional woundings that our Indigo Children carry and manifest. We called the process *The 17: Spiritually Healing Children's Emotional Wounds.*

## Waiting and Wondering

Over and over again, we asked our Spiritual Guidance: "Shall we announce *The 17* to a much wider audience? Shall we start a full-time healing practice with *The 17*? Shall we train others to facilitate the process so that we can reach as many children as possible?" And over and over again, our Spiritual Guidance said to us: "Not yet. Not yet."

Over time, we got pretty confused and frustrated. We felt that we had been given a valuable and much-needed healing technique for our Indigo Children, and we knew that there are hundreds of thousands, millions of Indigo Children who are in emotional pain. And yet the very Spiritual Guidance that had given us this gift was not permitting us to use it to help bring healing. No matter how often we asked, we were told, "Not yet. Not yet."

Now, we have great trust in Guidance. We know that everything is perfect, and that the universe unfolds just as it should. We knew that if Guidance were telling us to wait, there must be good reason in the World of Spirit. But the constant sight of so many still-in-pain Indigo Children who would surely benefit from this process made the waiting very hard.

Yet during this time, Guidance was not silent. We received further instructions. We were told that Ellen would channel new, evolving, and ever-growing information about the Indigos and about *The 17*. Wayne would be the public spokesman about the process and play the YOUMEES with the children and their parents.

## TELLING

Still, we waited to be told when we could make *The 17* healing process public and give it over to as many children as possible. Finally, on Sunday morning, March 4, 2001, Guidance said to Wayne: "Now. Now is the time. Get ready to announce *The 17*. Get ready to tell about the spiritual healing for the children."

For a number of years, Ellen had been holding a monthly Thursday evening Gathering to share the spiritual information for us and for our world that she had been given from Guidance during the past month. Scores of people always attended these Gatherings, so that they could hear the channeled teachings and enrich their own lives. Since so many of these folks are deeply involved in the World of Spirit, we thought that this would be the perfect group to be the first to hear about *The 17*.

We decided that at the next Gathering, scheduled for Thursday, March 15, 2001, Wayne would talk about the Indigo Children and announce the existence of the guided spiritual healing process, *The 17*. He would prepare some written materials that people could take with them, describing the principles and the process of *The 17*, and information about how to schedule a healing session.

On Monday, March 5, 2001—the very day after we had been told that the time had finally come to announce the healing process—right here in Santee, California, a suburb of San Diego, a 15-year-old boy named Charles "Andy" Williams walked into Santana High School, and shot and killed two of his fellow students and wounded 13 others.

In the shadow of this tragedy, we realized why Guidance told us to reveal *The 17* at this time. In case there were any doubt about the depth of the emotional pain and existential angst that our Indigo Children can experience, the horrific shooting was an immediate, vivid, graphic, and frightening illustration. When no one seems to understand, when he/she has seemingly nowhere to turn and no way to salve the emotional and spiritual anguish, in the extreme, an Indigo Child may play out the great pain by bringing guns to school and killing classmates.

Ten days later, when Wayne spoke of the Indigo Children to the people at Ellen's Gathering, most nodded in sad recognition of the often-painful Earth-existence of our Indigo Children, and most were very pleased to learn that a new, spiritual healing process is now available.

# Me, Too

Right after the public announcement of *The 17*, three things happened. First, parents began making appointments for YOUMEE sessions for their children, and more and more Indigo Children began to experience the effects of spiritual healing.

Then, we began hearing from parents of children who are younger than age seven about the emotional pain their children were experiencing.

Sadly, we could not help them. Guidance had been specific. *The 17* is for children seven to seventeen years of age. But persistent—and scared—parents of the young ones kept asking. Especially after an essay that Wayne had written was published in a popular Indigo book, we began getting calls and e-mails from all over the world. "Please find a way to help my little Indigo Child who is in such pain." We begged—yes, we literally begged—our Spiritual Guidance for a solution.

Guidance heard our cries. We were given a spiritual healing process for Indigo children from birth to age seven. We call it *GraceLight: Weaving Harmony for the Littlest Indigos.* As soon as *GraceLight* was available, we offered it to the parents who had contacted us about their young children. Moms and dads now tell of little ones who seem much more comfortable and content.

Then, we began hearing from adults—people older than seventeen years of age—who said, "What about me? I resonate completely with all the Indigo characteristics and feelings that you describe. The behaviors are very familiar. I would like a spiritual healing for myself. Yet you said that the process is only for those up to age seventeen. Don't you have a healing process for me, too?"

Wayne understood. For he sensed—and his Spiritual Guidance confirmed—that he is an Adult Indigo who would greatly benefit from spiritual healing process. So, again, we went to Guidance, and Guidance finally revealed a spiritual healing for Adult Indigos—Indigo Children whose spiritual woundings of childhood went unhealed and were carried over to adulthood. We call this healing *The Point of Essence Process: Pro-Claiming the Truth of Who You Are.*

Many, many adults have already benefited from *The Point of Essence Process*, reporting that parts of themselves that have been hidden away almost all their lives are now opening and flowing. And we can offer personal testimony to the effectiveness of this process, for we can clearly see that Wayne's own life has been inspirited and enriched by this spiritual healing.

# AND NOW

Since that time in early 2001, Wayne has facilitated *The 17* and *GraceLight* sessions for hundreds and hundreds of Indigo Children and their parents, and he has facilitated hundreds of *Point of Essence* sessions for Adult Indigos. We have been the humble and grateful witnesses to the awesome healing power of these sacred processes.

We continue to get new, evolving information from Guidance that refines the three processes and makes them even more powerfully effective.

To most effectively spread the word about spiritual healing for Indigo Children and Adult Indigos, we established The Soul Center for Spiritual Healing.

As the logo for our literature and brochures, we chose the spiral, because it represents for us evolution and transformation.

At the end of each *17* session, in addition to an Earth-stone, which effectively supports the integration of healing, we give each child a little brass spiral as a remembrance of playing the YOUMEES.

We also give a spiral to all the parents who have *GraceLight* sessions of behalf of their children and to all the Adult Indigos who have a *Point of Essence* session. We have been told that the little brass spiral has become some children's "most priceless possession."

We set up a toll free telephone number—**1-877-SOUL-KID**—so that parents who needed information about spiritual healing could get it without incurring any expense, and so that the children with whom Wayne played the YOUMEES could call anytime "just to talk."

We set up a Website—**www.soulbysoul.com**—to give information about spiritual healings for Indigos to a wide international audience.

We established a program to train and certify Facilitators from all around the country, who take these spiritual healings back to their local communities and reach out to as many Indigos as possible.

Yet we know that no matter how much information we can give out by telephone and Internet, and no matter how many Facilitators we are able to train, we will never be able to personally reach the hundreds of thousands, the millions of Indigo Children and Adult Indigos who would greatly benefit from these processes. So, we decided to write a practical guide and handbook for spiritually healing Indigo Children and Adult Indigos.

The book gives step-by-step instructions for each process, so that a parent can facilitate *The 17* or *GraceLight* for his/her own children, and so that Adult Indigos can facilitate *The Point of Essence Process* for themselves.

It is our fondest hope that this book will bring the possibility of spiritual healing to every Indigo who needs and wants it.

## CHILDREN OF SPIRIT

During the development of *The 17*, Wayne sensed that the process inherently holds its own rhythm, its own melody. He sensed that the words and the music to the melody are ancient and deeply embedded in Indigo souls. His search for song led him to the first verse of the 14th chapter of the biblical book of Deuteronomy.

He slightly modified the text so that it becomes universal and put the words to a sweet, gentle old prayer-song.

In Hebrew, the words are, *Banim Atem LaShem.* Universally translated, they are, "You are Children of Spirit."

Wayne began singing these melodic words to each child at the conclusion of a *17* session. The same thing happened almost every time. For a few seconds, the children's eyes darted back and forth, as if mind-heart were searching for something that was once known and comfortably familiar, but that has not been heard for a very, very long time. Very soon, the children's eyes "locked in," and a calm, peaceful look came on their faces. They often swayed slightly to the old, old words and melody that they were hearing again. When the song was finished, they smiled slightly. Some seemed lost in the far-away. Others nodded in deep remembrance. Others, in the quietest and most gentle voice, said, "Thank you."

The children know: They are Children of Spirit.

Soon, Wayne began singing the same song to Adult Indigos who came for a *Point of Essence* session, for after all, they are Children of Spirit, now grown up, but always Children of Spirit.

We made an audiotape of the song, so that our Indigo Children and Adult Indigos can continually hear the words and the melody, and make them their own.

Our work with the Indigos convinces us: The Indigo Children and Adult Indigos are, indeed, Children of Spirit.

We humbly and gratefully give thanks to Guidance for giving us this surprisingly unexpected but deeply satisfying mission, of working with these extraordinary Indigo souls.

And we greatly honor Indigos for their courage to spiritually heal, and we joyfully celebrate them as they fulfill their vision and lead us home to a world of transformation and perfection.

# Accompaniment

## II

# EXPLAINING SOUL MEMORY DISCOVERY

SOUL MEMORY DISCOVERY is a spiritual healing modality that enables us to access, identify, and release troubling issues that limit our lives and inhibit the full expression of our Essence and our Beings.

Soul Memory Discovery is helpful in healing emotional challenges, such as depression, anxiety, phobias, rage, fears, schizophrenia, and bipolar disorder. It has helped people move through and heal physical ailments, such as arthritis, asthma, headaches, digestive disorders, cystic fibrosis, cancer, immune disorders, seizure disorders, and addictions. It can be helpful in shifting life challenges, such as problematic relationships, aloneness and isolation, poverty and lack, feelings of being lost and stuck, empty and meaningless.

The foundational theory of Soul Memory Discovery is that our bodies hold memories of everything that has ever happened to us in this lifetime. We know that all of our experiences in this lifetime are recorded somewhere in our physical selves.

Our language expresses this wisdom so eloquently: We speak of having a "broken heart," and of "sitting on our anger," and of "not being able to stomach it," and of "shouldering a burden."

And, of course, we know that everything that happens to us is recorded in our brains—as on a continuously running tape or film—whether or not we are consciously aware of it.

Just as our bodies hold memories of everything that has happened to us in this lifetime, so our auras, our electro-magnetic fields around our bodies, hold memories of everything that has ever happened to our souls.

If we think of the soul as that eternal part of us that will continue on long after we are finished with these bodies, then it makes sense to think that these souls must have been doing something before they came into these bodies as well.

Some of us believe that these souls were in other bodies other lifetimes. Others believe that these souls were, perhaps, in other forms in other worlds. Some believe that souls stay in the Higher Realms with God until they are called to be in this one body in this one lifetime. Whatever our belief, our souls come to us with their own histories, and we carry the memories of those histories in our auric fields.

When we do a polarity balance that is specific to Soul Memory Discovery work and co-create Sacred Space, we are able to access all those memory banks stored in our body and in our auric field. What is wonderful about accessing these memory banks is that we can then find the origin of any issue, or any complex of symptoms—be it a physical, emotional, or spiritual issue, or even life patterns, or work habits, or entire belief systems.

Unlike traditional talk therapy, where it can take months or even years to find the origins of an issue, understand those originating events, and move through the healing, with the Soul Memory Discovery Process, we can access the origins of an issue almost immediately and effortlessly. The information comes when the Soul Memory Facilitator and the client together ask questions of the client's own soul and Spiritual Guidance Team. We are spiritually directed, and given access to, the specific information necessary to release the issue which holds the symptoms in place.

Once we find the originating events of the current issue, there is a very simple release process, which lifts those origins out of the system. This process is swift, gentle, and sacred. Once the symptoms are no longer being sourced, they dry up and they go away.

All of this is accomplished in one two to three hour session.

Soul Memory Discovery is "sacred ritual" that uses the power of language and of specially spoken words to shift energy and effect change. It is a tremendously efficient and effective spiritual healing process.

We not only have memories of traumatic events stored in our auric field, but we also hold memories of all the spiritual contracts we have ever made. In a Soul Memory Discovery session, we can also access those contracts and agreements, and receive information about our chosen mission and purpose in this lifetime.

For example, we can look at the contracts we made to partner in this lifetime with particular people, including our parents, our spouses, our children, or any of our significant others.

We can look at our career paths, our spiritual paths, our relationships with teachers and guides, colleagues and associates, friends and foes. It can be very helpful to see these contracts and to become conscious of the ways Spirit attempts to guide and direct us. We can also come to know our Guides, MasterGuides, and Guardian Angels, who have contracted to serve with us in this lifetime and support us in our evolution.

We are very blessed to be in body at this time. Each of us is here because of the unique contributions we are able to make to our world. We are being called forward to stand in the fullness of our Essences, to be the largest expressions of ourselves. We no longer have the luxury of carrying debilitating symptoms, which limit the expression of our GodSelves. And we no longer have the luxury of sitting in therapy for months or years trying to heal ourselves. The time demands that we be what we came here to be and do what we came here to do. Our world demands our full presence—now.

Soul Memory Discovery is a great gift for us. It allows us to lift off limitation and, almost immediately, to step into the fullness of our Truths in life-affirming, grace-filled ways.

Then, we can be what we truly came here to be—God's partners in designing and co-creating a Garden of Eden on this Earth.

*"I Am That I Am"*

# ABOUT THE AUTHORS

RABBI WAYNE DOSICK, PH.D., D.D., is an educator, writer, spiritual guide, and healer who teaches and counsels about faith and spirit, ethical values, life transformations, and evolving human consciousness.

He is the founder and spiritual leader of The Elijah Minyan; an adjunct professor at the University of San Diego; and the award-winning author of six books, including the highly acclaimed and much beloved *Golden Rules: The Ten Ethical Values Parents Need to Teach Their Children.*

Dr. Dosick is a popular speaker and seminar leader who has spoken to more than 200 audiences throughout the country and has been interviewed on more than 150 radio and television shows. Articles about him and his books have appeared in more than 85 newspapers and periodicals.

Dr. Dosick has taught youngsters from pre-school through college and graduate school; counseled at summer camps; directed day and supplementary schools, and youth programs; and conducted seminars and retreats for children of all ages and their parents.

He now directs The Soul Center for Spiritual Healing, home of *The 17, GraceLight,* and *The Point of Essence Process.*

Rabbi Dosick has been called "one of the most gifted teachers of our generation who understands the mindset, needs, and yearnings of people, and responds to this intellectual and inner searching in peerless fashion."

He is, himself, an Adult Indigo, whose life has been inspirited and enriched by these sacred processes.

These spiritual healings are the project of his heart and the mission of his soul.

ELLEN KAUFMAN DOSICK, MSW, LCSW, with degrees from the University of Chicago, has been a practicing psychotherapist for more than 25 years. She has served on the faculty of the University of Southern California School of Social Work, and directed social service programs and offices.

She has taught children and their parents at every level; directed school, after-school, and summer programs; and directed Children's Community Theater.

Ms. Kaufman Dosick practices Soul Memory Discovery, a healing therapy, which she finds the most effective tool for human development and change.

She is the World Master Teacher who trains and certifies Soul Memory Discovery Facilitators from around the country.

She publishes a bi-monthly "Gathering Transmission," which brings channeled messages from her Spiritual Guidance to our world and us. These transmissions are so informative and accurate that they have been dubbed "Spiritual Headline News."

The "Gathering Transmission" is available by e-mail or surface mail subscription, and the collected *Gathering Transmissions* from the years 1998-2002 are available in booklet form.

For her deep connection to Spirit and her incisive insights into the human psyche and the cosmos in which we live, Ellen has been called "a modern-day prophet."


Wayne and Ellen live in La Costa, California, where their home is a center for prayer, learning, and healing; and a community gathering place for Light-workers and spiritual seekers.

For additional information, please go to these Websites:

# www.healingtheindigo.com
# www.soulbysoul.com

For information about booking a speaking engagement or seminar, please call Jodere Group at 1-800-569-1002.

We hope this Jodere Group book has benefited you in your quest for personal, intellectual, and spiritual growth.

Jodere Group is passionate about bringing new and exciting books, such as *Spiritually Healing the Indigo Children*, to readers worldwide. Our company was created as a unique publishing and multimedia avenue for individuals whose mission it is to impact the lives of others positively. We recognize the strength of an original thought, a kind word, and a selfless act—and the power of the individuals who possess them. We are committed to providing the support, passion, and creativity necessary for these individuals to achieve their goals and dreams.

Jodere Group is comprised of a dedicated and creative group of people who strive to provide the highest quality of books, audio programs, online services, and live events to people who pursue life-long learning. It is our personal and professional commitment to embrace our authors, speakers, and readers with helpfulness, respect, and enthusiasm.

For more information about our products, authors, or live events, please call **800.569.1002** or visit us on the Web at **www.jodere.com**.